Draw Close

Books by Willard F. Harley, Jr.

His Needs, Her Needs, Revised and Expanded Edition
Love Busters, Revised and Expanded Edition
Five Steps to Romantic Love
Fall in Love, Stay in Love
His Needs, Her Needs for Parents
Surviving an Affair
Trading Dead-End Relationships for Lasting Love
I Promise You
Effective Marriage Counseling

Draw Close

A Devotional for Couples

Willard F. Harley, Jr.
and Joyce S. Harley

Revell

a division of Baker Publishing Group
Grand Rapids, Michigan

Published by Revell
a division of Baker Publishing Group
P.O. Box 6287, Grand Rapids, MI 49516-6287
www.revellbooks.com

Printed in the United States of America

Library of Congress Cataloging-in-Publication Data
Harley, Willard F.
    Draw close: a devotional for couples / Willard F. Harley, Jr. and Joyce S. Harley.
        p.   cm.
    ISBN 978-0-8007-2005-6 (cloth)
    ISBN 978-0-8007-2098-8 (pbk.)
    1. Spouses—Prayers and devotions. 2. Marriage—Religious aspects—Christianity—
Prayers and devotions. I. Harley, Joyce. II. Title.
BV4596.M3.H38 2011
242'644—dc23   2011018067

To protect the privacy of those who have shared their stories with the author, some details and names have been changed.

11 12 13 14 15 16 17   7 6 5 4 3 2 1

We wish to thank our niece, Kathryn Brown Treick, for her valuable assistance in helping us write this book. With all you've accomplished, including your recent graduate studies and research, we're sure we'll be seeing your name in more books in the future.

And many thanks to Jennifer Leep, editorial director of Revell, for your editorial savvy and many hours of hard work that helped make this book possible. Words cannot say how much we appreciate you and the rest of the dedicated staff at Revell.

Contents

Contents

Introduction

Getting the Most from This Devotional

We have written this book to help you achieve two very important goals: to draw you closer to the Lord and to draw you closer to each other. In our own forty-eight years of marriage, these two goals have been the highest priorities of our lives and they have supported each other—the closer we have been to the Lord the easier it has been to be close to each other, and the closer we have been to each other the easier it has been to be close to the Lord.

God's purpose for marriage, that two become one, is an analogy of our relationship with him. God wants a husband and wife to be bonded to each other in the same way we are to be bonded with him. He wants an exclusive relationship with us in the same way a marriage is to be exclusive. The commandment to have no other gods before him (Exod. 20:3) is closely related to the commandment not to commit adultery (Exod. 20:14).

God has given us a powerful incentive to fulfill his purpose for marriage: an incredible attraction for each other that we call romantic love. It's a litmus test of a couple's care for each other. When they provide to each other the quality of care that God intended in marriage, they experience romantic love throughout life, the way we've experienced it. But when they don't provide that care for each other, they lose that feeling of love.

Each chapter opens with Scripture to be discussed that week. Then there are five short sections that are to be read by both of you together during each of the first five days of the week. There is also a prayer at the end of each chapter you can pray together after you read each section. On the sixth day of each week, we suggest you review the lesson of that week and discuss how you will apply it to your marriage.

The lessons in this book cover just about every challenge couples face in marriage, and they give you solutions that will help you grow in compatibility and mutual care. Each daily segment can be read in about five minutes and is designed to help remind you of the value of your marriage and your relationship with God. But if you have been struggling with the issue introduced by a certain lesson, take more time each day to consider ways to apply the solutions we suggest. You may also find it helpful to extend that particular lesson beyond a single week.

Your marriage is very important to God. He has joined you together so that you will care for each other (Matt. 19:6). If you follow his will for your marriage, it will be romantic, passionate, and very fulfilling for both of you.

Week 1

A Delightful Love

Let him kiss me with the kisses of his mouth—
for your love is more delightful than wine . . .
Take me away with you—let us hurry!
Let the king bring me into his chambers.

Song of Songs 1:2, 4

When Matt and Ellie were first married, their friends teased them about their open affection for each other. Behind closed doors, they couldn't get enough of each other. Theirs was a passionate marriage, and they took great pleasure in expressing their love for one another every way they could.

Three children and eight years later, their passion seemed like a dim candle, not a blazing fire. They had stopped "dating" each other right around the birth of their second child, and now it felt as if every ounce of energy was devoted to work, children, housekeeping, and a myriad of other responsibilities. Ellie usually stumbled off to bed exhausted after a long day with the kids, while Matt caught *Sports Center* after everyone else was asleep. Sometimes they would laugh about it; they loved their children dearly, but had no idea how much work raising them would turn out to be. They missed the freedom and spontaneity they had in the first year of their marriage before their first child, Jill, arrived. Now it seemed they didn't have the time or energy for the passion that was once an essential part of their relationship.

Day 1

God devoted an entire book of the Bible to poetry describing a passionate marriage—that's how important it is to him. He designed marriage to be passionate and fulfilling. If you've only read Song of Songs allegorically in the past, do yourselves a favor: read it with each other in mind. Take a few moments today and flip through the eight chapters of this sensual book. Which verses stand out to you? Any surprises? What are some of the aspects of marriage that are celebrated by the couple in Song of Songs?

The truth is that you can, and should, have a passionate marriage for your entire lifetime together. We've experienced that passion with each other for forty-eight years now—and it's not over yet. Romance is something that should never end in marriage. God intended that you love each other passionately, regardless of the number of children you have or any of the other responsibilities you will face. In this book, we'll share with you what we have done to keep our marriage passionate and full of romance for all these years. And we'll show you how you've been created by God to have that kind of marriage too.

Day 2

What is passion? It's the feeling of love—romantic love. When a husband and wife feel an incredible attraction for each other, they have that special feeling. They're in love.

To understand where this kind of love comes from, think of your feelings like a bank—a Love Bank in this case. Each of you has an account in the other's Love Bank, and every interaction with each other strengthens or weakens your relationship by making either a deposit or a withdrawal from those accounts. The better you feel during an interaction, the more "love units" are deposited in your spouse's account. The worse you feel, the more are withdrawn.

When you were dating each other, no doubt you both made an effort to make as many deposits as possible with every conversation and activity you had together, even though you may not have thought of it in those terms. You also minimized withdrawals by avoiding conflicts and arguments. Initially, that created moderately high Love Bank balances in each other's accounts, which caused you to feel attracted to each other—you liked each other.

As your balances kept rising, they eventually breached what we call the romantic love threshold, and your emotions intensified—you fell *in love*.

Think back to those dating days. Do you remember how it felt to fall in love with each other for the first time? This week, consider how you can feed each other's Love Banks the same way you did when you first met.

Day 3

Unfortunately what goes up can also go down. If, at any point, the two of you stop making deposits and start making withdrawals, your Love Bank balances will be in danger of dropping below the romantic love threshold, leaving you with a feeling of attraction but no longer feeling in love. If you continue to drain each other's accounts, letting the balances fall to zero, you'll eventually feel nothing toward each other. And if you let withdrawals continue until you both have negative balances, a feeling of repulsion will start to emerge. The once happy couple you used to be will seem a distant memory.

The good news is, that doesn't have to happen. In the coming weeks we'll show you how to keep making deposits and avoiding withdrawals—so that you, too, will experience the kind of marriage that we have had for forty-eight years.

Imagine, after fifteen—or fifty—years of marriage, still feeling the passionate love reflected in Song of Songs, where the husband says to his wife,

> You have stolen my heart, my sister, my bride;
>   you have stolen my heart
> with one glance of your eyes,
>   with one jewel of your necklace. . . .
> How much more pleasing is your love than wine,
>   and the fragrance of your perfume than any spice! (4:9–10)

Reflect on these words for a moment. The lover feels that his heart has been stolen away by his wife. Just one glance from her melts his heart. He finds great delight in her love, and it pleases him more than wine. Even her scent drives him crazy.

Day 4

While Song of Songs is the most explicit book in Scripture about passionate marriage, it is by no means the only word God has given us on the fulfilling marriage relationship. Indeed, in the book of Proverbs, we find a beautiful blessing:

> May your fountain be blessed,
>   and may you rejoice in the wife of your youth.
> A loving doe, a graceful deer—
>   may her breasts satisfy you always,
>   may you ever be captivated by her love. (5:18–19)

It appears these verses are directed to someone who has already been married for some time—the speaker blesses the hearer by asking for blessings on his "fountain" and that he will "rejoice in the wife of your youth." Most likely this couple was not young anymore! But the husband could still "ever be captivated by her love." A lifetime of love is not wishful thinking; it's reality for couples who have learned to keep their Love Bank balances high.

Many don't believe that a lifetime of passion is really possible—instead they buy into the idea that romance and passion will inevitably fade. But our own personal experience is living proof that they're wrong. We have stayed *in love* with each other throughout our entire marriage. And we're not alone. Our parents experienced the same thing. In fact, about 20 percent of all marriages remain passionate for a lifetime. These are the couples who keep their promises to please each other and avoid hurting each other. It's not some closely guarded secret—it's what couples expect from each other. And it's what God expects of you too.

Day 5

Song of Songs gives us a beautiful picture of what romantic love looks like. Skim it again: what words stand out to you? Write those words on a sheet of paper and share them with each other.

We are struck by words such as "delightful," "pleasing," "beautiful," "darling," "charming"—this is a couple that clearly feels romantic love. Are these words that you would use to describe each other or your marriage? Do you have a good feeling when you think about each other? Would you rather be with each other than anyone else? Do you enjoy telling each other your deepest feelings and most private experiences? Do you feel "chemistry" together? Does your spouse bring out the best in you? These are some questions that get to the essence of what the feeling of romantic love really is. And they offer an indication of how well you're doing at maintaining healthy Love Bank balances with each other.

Before the week ends, think back over the past few days. What was the biggest "deposit" each of you made into each other's Love

Banks? Were there any major "withdrawals"? Talk about ways you can make more deposits and fewer withdrawals in the coming week.

Remember, romantic love doesn't have to fade away with time. You can be as much in love with each other fifty years from now as you are today.

⤳⟳⟲ PRAYER FOR THE WEEK ⟳⟲⟳

Lord, we want to have a passionate marriage that is characterized by love for each other and delight in each other. We know it's possible because you have said so in your Word. So we ask you to help us become more sensitive to each other, to help us avoid hurting each other, and to help us find fulfillment in each other. Help us to be intentional in seeking out ways to demonstrate our care for one another. Lead us by your Holy Spirit, so that our marriage will honor and glorify you.

Week 2

Loving Is Caring

Love is patient, love is kind. It does not envy, it does not boast, it is not proud. It does not dishonor others, it is not self-seeking, it is not easily angered, it keeps no record of wrongs.

1 Corinthians 13:4–5

Helen will never forget the night that Aaron told her he loved her for the first time. It had been a wonderful date, ending with a long twilight walk home through their favorite park. They admired the twinkling lights of the city as they strolled hand in hand. They paused to gaze out over the river, and Aaron slipped his arms around Helen's waist. "I care about you," he whispered. She was confused. What did that mean? Was he trying to say that he was in love with her, or did he simply care for her the way a brother would care for his sister? Aaron sensed her bewilderment, and immediately straightened out the misunderstanding. "I am crazy about you, Helen. I can't stop thinking about you. I'm in love."

Aaron's actions backed up those words. In the few weeks they'd been dating, Aaron had found numerous ways to show how much he cared for Helen. He looked out for her. He applauded her successes and listened when she was having a hard time. And when they were together, she knew she had his undivided attention. Helen also cared for Aaron and her actions proved it as well. She gave him her undivided attention when they were together and listened attentively when he described both his achievements and his problems. She was an affectionate and enthusiastic companion, and always looked her best when she was with him. The care Aaron and Helen showed each other translated into massive Love Bank deposits that, in turn, triggered the love Aaron declared for Helen that night.

Day 1

Are you in love with each other, or do you merely care for each other? Despite Helen's initial disappointment with Aaron's first statement, care is not at all trivial in marriage. In fact, it's essential in creating romantic love. It's the care you show each other that makes Love Bank deposits and helps keep your balances above the romantic love threshold.

You see, there are two different types of love that are highly related to each other in marriage. Last week we looked at romantic love—that feeling of incredible attraction for someone of the opposite sex. Caring love, on the other hand, is a decision to take time and make an effort to make someone happy, and to do what you can to avoid making them unhappy. While romantic love is a feeling, caring love is a decision.

When we use the word *care* we're talking about what you *do* for each other, not how you *hope* or *feel*. When you married, you promised to keep caring for each other, and you promised to do things that would enhance the quality and enjoyment of each other's lives, just as you had done while you were dating. How well have you been keeping that promise lately? That's our focus for this week.

Day 2

So, what does caring love look like? First Corinthians 13:4–5 provides a good starting point. It lists some of the characteristics of caring love. To put it into action, let's consider these verses in more active terms: Love is *being patient*, love is *being kind*. Love is *not being envious, not boasting, not being proud*. Love is *not being rude* and *not looking out only for yourself*. Love is *not being easily angered* and *not keeping track of how the other person has wronged you*.

Most of the illustrations of caring love found in this Scripture focus attention on what love is not—what to avoid. Don't be envious, boastful, proud, rude, only looking out for yourself, easily angered, or always keeping track of the way the other person has wronged you. We'll talk about these "Love Busters," as we call them, in a few weeks.

But this week we want to address *positive* aspects of caring. In what ways should you be patient with each other? How does patience reflect your care? Caring love is patient with someone in ways that make them feel loved.

What about being kind? How do you express your kindness for each other? Do you make large Love Bank deposits with your kindness? Before you were married, your kindness was so effective that you fell in love with each other. But do you know exactly what you did to deposit so many love units—and what you must do to continue depositing them?

Spend some time today considering those questions. If you're not sure how to answer them right now, we'll help you think them through in the weeks to come.

Day 3

When you come right down to it, the promise you made to care for each other when you married is a promise to try to make each other happy and avoid making each other unhappy. As we saw in

1 Corinthians 13:4–5, care consists of these two objectives—what to do and what not to do.

This week we're focusing on the care that's required to make each other happy. It's care that's directed at what we call an "emotional need." *An emotional need is a craving that when met leaves us feeling happy and content, and when unmet leaves us feeling unhappy and frustrated.* Can you think of something that makes you feel good when you have it, and makes you feel frustrated when you don't? Do you ever have a craving for it? If so, it's one of your emotional needs.

You have thousands of emotional needs because there are thousands of ways to make you feel good. But not all emotional needs are the same. When some are met you feel okay, but when others are met you feel fantastic. Some result in moderate Love Bank deposits while others translate to massive deposits. We call those needs that make the largest deposits the *most important emotional needs*.

You both have emotional needs. If you discover and learn to meet those that are most important to each of you, you will be demonstrating the kind of caring love for each other that triggers romantic love. Meeting each other's most important emotional needs is the essence of your caring love for each other.

Day 4

How do you discover each other's most important emotional needs? Well, here's a place to start: Ask each other to explain what would make you the happiest if someone were to do it for you, and the most frustrated if they didn't do it. To qualify, you must have a craving for it—you want it so badly you can almost taste it. Pause for a moment. How would you answer that question? Think for a moment about the last time your spouse did something for you that made you feel terrific. Did you crave what it was? Would you have been frustrated if your spouse didn't do it?

When I first started asking this question to couples I counseled, I didn't know what the answers would be—and didn't want to guess. But after asking hundreds of men and women, a pattern began to emerge. Almost everyone gave answers that could be classified into one or more of a list of ten categories: admiration, affection, conversation, domestic support, family commitment, financial support, honesty and openness, physical attractiveness, recreational companionship, and sexual fulfillment.

As you read that list of categories, which ones stand out to you? As you answer the questions at the beginning of this day's reading, identifying your emotional needs to each other, do any of them fit into these ten categories? Each of you should make your own list of emotional need categories that are most important to you. Share those lists with each other and you'll be on your way to understanding how to care for each other.

Day 5

When you compared your lists of emotional need categories yesterday, how well did they match? If you're like most couples, you may have seen some categories overlapping, but there was probably a significant difference as well.

Along with the discovery of a list of common emotional needs, I have also realized something else in my counseling of couples that helps make sense of why husbands and wives might have trouble making each other happy. When asked to prioritize these ten emotional needs, men tend to list them one way and women the opposite way. The five listed as most important by men are usually the five least important for women, and vice versa.

That means if you follow the Golden Rule—doing for each other what you wish your spouse would do for you—you often miss the mark. Doing for your spouse what you appreciate most is not necessarily what your spouse appreciates most. So if you want to make the largest Love Bank deposits, don't assume the two of you have the same most important emotional needs. Instead, first discover what they are and then learn to meet them for each other.

In the coming weeks, we'll address each of these needs in more detail so that you'll learn to become experts in caring for each other. But for now, focus your attention on identifying your five most important emotional needs that when met would make you happiest, and when unmet would make you most frustrated. And start thinking of ways you can care for each other by meeting those needs this week.

⟶ PRAYER FOR THE WEEK ⟵

Lord, we want to demonstrate our love for each other with patience and kindness. Help us to discover each other's most important emotional needs and learn to meet them for each other. Help us to avoid being envious, boastful, proud, rude, looking out only for ourselves, easily angered, or always keeping track of the ways we have wronged each other. We ask you to guide us by your Holy Spirit and to give us greater sensitivity toward each other.

Week 3

Time Matters

As Jesus and his disciples were on their way, he came to a village where a woman named Martha opened her home to him. She had a sister called Mary, who sat at the Lord's feet listening to what he said. But Martha was distracted by all the preparations that had to be made. She came to him and asked, "Lord, don't you care that my sister has left me to do the work by myself? Tell her to help me!"

"Martha, Martha," the Lord answered, "you are worried and upset about many things, but only one thing is needed. Mary has chosen what is better, and it will not be taken away from her."

Luke 10:38–42

Brian and Sarah feel the pressure of urgency every day in their marriage. There never seems to be enough time. Their children need to be driven to practices, games, and lessons; work pressures lead to long hours; and household chores seem to be never-ending.

Brian's saving grace is a weekly golf game with his buddies that helps him escape from all the pressure he feels. And Sarah meets with a few friends regularly for a well-deserved outing as well. These activities help keep them both sane—they need the time to relax. Unfortunately, it seems they have no time to relax with each other.

Day 1

Imagine the scene: Martha has the honor of welcoming Jesus and his friends into her home for dinner. So much to prepare! She was buzzing around in the kitchen, making sure everything would be perfect. It was a lot of work. And then she catches a glimpse of her sister—there's Mary, sitting with Jesus and his friends, hanging on his every word. And Martha was incensed. She finally explodes, "Jesus, don't you even care about me? Mary's just sitting there and I am doing ALL the work!" Okay, that's a paraphrase, but you get the idea. Martha is consumed by what needs to be done, and she is beyond annoyed that her sister isn't helping.

Jesus comes back with a gentle response. He notes that Martha is "worried and upset about many things," but turns her eyes to what should be her top priority: listening to him. Would Jesus have been content with a meal that was less elaborate if it meant that Martha, too, could sit there at his feet? I doubt Jesus would have reprimanded his dear Martha for such a decision.

It's easy to let the urgent take precedence over the important. What we consider to be an emergency can often turn out to be a distraction from what really should be done. And, sadly, this happens all too often in marriages. As we begin this week, consider the last time you let the tyranny of the urgent take your focus off your marriage. What would it look like to make your marriage your top priority this week?

Day 2

How much time did you spend together as a dating couple? What did you do with that time? If you are like most couples, you spent at least fifteen hours each week together, in person or on the telephone, and you used that time to meet each other's most important emotional needs. That's what it takes to create and maintain a romantic relationship: enough time to make large Love Bank deposits.

Your time together isn't determined by chance. Before you were married, you made spending as much time together as possible a high priority by putting each other into your schedules—you made dates to be together. And you may well have looked forward to being able to spend even more time together as a married couple. But unless you make a conscious effort to keep scheduling that time, you'll find that it will slip away and you'll neglect each other, just as Martha neglected Jesus.

I have done considerable research into the amount of time a couple must spend together to stay in love. That research has included not only dating couples, but also married couples and even couples having affairs. Remember the amount of time we mentioned above when you thought back to your dating days? Back then you likely spent at least fifteen hours a week giving each other undivided attention. And it turns out that's the same amount of time it takes for the average couple to sustain a romantic relationship.

How much time did you spend alone together during the past week? Do you need to make some adjustments to carve out fifteen hours a week for each other? That's our focus for this week.

Day 3

Unless you schedule time together as a couple, something far less important will always take its place.

You might think it seems contrived to actually schedule time to meet each other's most important emotional needs, but again, think back to when you dated. That's precisely how it happened then: you scheduled time to be with each other.

Now that you're married and are together every day, it's easy to assume such scheduling isn't required, that simply being in the house together or being asleep in bed together will get the job done. But it's not so. Only when you give each other your *undivided* attention are you able to meet the needs that make the largest Love Bank deposits. And you won't find that time unless it's planned.

When you married, you promised to care for each other in joy and in sorrow, in sickness and in health, in plenty and in want, as long as you both shall live. What that really means is you promised each other *romance* in spite of your circumstances. You committed to exclusively fulfill each other's most important emotional needs, and you didn't say "until children or other distractions do us part." So to fulfill that commitment, schedule the time to do it.

Day 4

When Martha was consumed with anxiety and stress over the many preparations she had in front of her, Jesus refocused her attention. He told her that only one thing was necessary. She had been unable to see what was important because she had been too focused on the many things she thought needed to be done. She missed out on what *actually* needed to be done. This same principle applies in marriage.

Do you see time spent with each other as a necessity? We want you to look at your appointment book, calendar, BlackBerry, iPhone—wherever you keep your appointments. Is there any evidence there that time with each other is a high priority for you? Your calendar usually reflects your priorities.

If the two of you have not made your time together your highest priority, you may not be seeing the success of your marriage as a "necessary thing," worthy of your attention. The clutter in your schedule may be so overwhelming you have come to the conclusion that your time together is a luxury you simply can't afford right now. If that's the case, we highly recommend you make a date for 3:30 on Sunday afternoon to schedule fifteen hours together this week. The time you spend reading this book and following our other recommendations can count toward that time together. How would that work for you? Can you afford to give each other the time it takes to care for each other? We promise you won't regret it.

───── Day 5 ─────

Bob and Laura used to let life happen to them, until one day they woke up and found themselves so overextended that they were both stressed out of their minds. So they sat down together over coffee one Saturday morning and talked—really talked. They made a list of all their commitments according to priority—which were most important, and which were least important.

Some activities were so unimportant that Bob and Laura agreed to simply let them go. They also found activities that were important but didn't have to interfere with their time together. For example, they decided to shift from separate Bible studies that met on opposite nights to a couples' Bible study they could attend together.

They decided that in the future each of their children would be limited to one sport or afterschool activity at a time. And despite the children's initial disappointment, the next season found them less stressed with more time for homework and friends. And Laura spent less time driving from one activity to another.

Bob and Laura took control of their schedule, and through prayer and reflection created a lifestyle that helped them achieve their highest priorities.

How about you? Consider all of your activities. Are they really necessary? Are you doing them to impress others or gain their approval? Are you finding you've simply gotten into a rut, doing the same things every week without any real purpose? Be honest with yourselves.

Next to time spent with God, the most important person you should be with is each other. It's his will for your life that you have a strong, passion-filled marriage. And you won't be able to achieve that goal if you don't schedule time to be together. So let him guide you to the best use of your time.

PRAYER FOR THE WEEK

Lord, we want to make each other a priority. Help us schedule time with each other, and use that time to care for each other. Thank you for giving us each other to care for, and help us provide that care with joy and enthusiasm. Help us set our minds on you as the center of our marriage and to follow your priorities. Our lives and our time are yours—please help us use them for your honor and glory.

Week 4

Two Became One

For this reason a man will leave his father and mother and be united to his wife, and they will become one flesh.

Genesis 2:24

It was going to be a beautiful moment in the wedding ceremony. Rachel had always wanted to light a "unity candle" at her wedding, symbolizing that in her marriage to Jason two were becoming one. But it wasn't until the moment they sat down with their wedding planner to go through the details of the ceremony that she really thought about its true meaning.

The wedding planner explained that the unity candle ceremony could be performed two ways. After the unity candle was lit, some blew out the two side candles as an expression of their new unity in marriage. But other couples left the side candles burning, indicating that, while united in marriage, they would still be retaining their individuality.

For Jason, it wasn't a big deal—leave the candles lit, blow them out—he didn't care. But this detail of the wedding ceremony got Rachel thinking: *Does marriage mean that I lose my identity? What am I getting myself into?*

Day 1

You may have had a unity candle at your wedding. And you may have left the side candles burning to emphasize your individuality or you may have blown them out to emphasize your new unity as husband and wife. But the real question is this: What does it mean that two become one? Are husband and wife two individuals living independent lives in the same house, honoring and encouraging each other when needed, but essentially separate? Or is a married couple some other entity?

To find the answer to this question, let's look at how Scripture describes marriage. We don't need to read very far to find the very first reference. Right after God had created the first woman, Eve, to accompany the first man, Adam, he defined the marriage relationship: "For this reason a man will leave his father and mother and be united to his wife, and they will become one flesh" (Gen. 2:24). According to this definition, a husband and wife are essentially and intimately connected, and it's for this reason the two become one. They are to leave their respective families and become a new family. They are to blend into each other to become a new entity. That's the definition of marriage—two becoming one.

Reflect for a few moments on this definition of marriage. Have the two of you become a new entity with each other? What does that mean in practical, day-to-day living?

Day 2

Joshua was newly married and his single friends were giving him a particularly hard time. You see, his wife, Stephanie, was a nurse, and she often worked until late in the evening. So Joshua generally headed out to grab dinner with his buddies after work and sometimes joined them for a game of pool afterward. But he always called Stephanie at her break time to check in and let her know where he was. Joshua's friends mocked him, remarking to each other that he was "whipped." But Joshua knew that Stephanie appreciated his calls and wouldn't let his friends' ridicule deter him from doing what he knew was right. He was beginning to understand why he needed friends who supported his marriage instead of those who would tempt him to ignore his wife's feelings.

When Joshua called Stephanie, he was being considerate of her feelings. He was aware of her needs and made an effort to fulfill those needs. If he had ignored her feelings, he would have been acting independently. But because he considered her feelings, even when they were not together, he was acting *interdependently*. And he wouldn't have had it any other way.

How about you? What would you do if you were in Joshua's shoes? Lots of voices might be ringing in your ear, much like Joshua's friends' voices did, tempting you to do your own thing without worrying about your spouse. But choosing to consider each other as well as yourself is *always* the best choice.

Day 3

When you stood before God and all of your family and friends to say "I do," you traded a life of independence for a life of interdependence. You may have had people depend on you before, but not in the same way you now depend on each other.

Every decision you make in married life affects each other. Your careers, finances, social circles, and every aspect of life are all intertwined. Where you choose to work, how you spend your money, whom you decide to be friends with—all of those things impact not only you but your spouse as well. You depend on each other to make wise choices in each of those areas so that your life together is secure and successful.

But it goes deeper than that. Not only do you depend on each other for all of those outward things, you also depend on each other for happiness and fulfillment. When you married, you promised to love, honor, and cherish each other—till death do you part. And you committed yourselves to caring for each other in ways that make each other feel happy and fulfilled.

That means recognizing your decisions *always* affect each other. How well are you doing at considering each other's feelings with every decision you make? If there are pockets of independence you're still clinging to in your marriage, it's time to replace those with the kind of interdependence that will allow your relationship to thrive.

Day 4

Joshua and Stephanie had discussed the issue of whether or not he should go out with his friends after work before he actually did it. Stephanie said it would be okay with her as long as he called her during her break. The call met her emotional need to have contact with him whenever possible. She didn't want his time with friends to interfere with an opportunity for them to talk to each other.

But consider the problems they would have had in their young marriage if Joshua followed his friends' advice to ignore her wishes to call during her break. Not only would he have missed a chance to meet Stephanie's need, but he also would have offended her. He would have communicated loud and clear that his friends were more important to him than she was.

Interdependent behavior is a way of saying, "I care about you. I want you to be happy, and I don't want to do anything that will hurt you." But it also communicates the importance of reciprocity in marriage. "I also want you to care about how I feel too. Let's do what works for both of us."

Have either of you made any decisions recently that benefited one of you at the other's expense? An offended spouse will know the answer to that question immediately, so ask each other right now if you have been acting independently. If so, make a commitment with each other that you will change that this week. Independence drains Love Bank balances, leading eventually to the kind of loveless marriage we are sure you don't want. However, when you become one in marriage you'll stay in love with each other, because interdependence makes deposits into *both* of your Love Banks simultaneously.

Day 5

As we've seen this week, the concept of interdependent behavior is rooted in the fact that you have become one as a married couple. You are now a new entity that does what is best for both of you. Paul explains it like this: "Husbands ought to love their wives as their own bodies. He who loves his wife loves himself. After all, no one ever hated his own body, but he feeds and cares for it, just as Christ does the church" (Eph. 5:28–29). That's a very practical observation. You already take care of yourself, but now that you and your spouse are one, you should also take care of your spouse. That means ensuring all of the decisions you make—both in their general outline and in the specifics—work for both of you.

Do you care for each other this way? Do you make decisions with each other's interests in mind, or do you find yourselves making independent decisions? Are you thoughtful or thoughtless when choices are to be made? Do you care for each other "as your own body?"

Paul says, "He who loves his wife loves himself." That goes for both of you. When you love your spouse, you love yourself, because you are a new entity now that you have become intertwined. Everything you do affects the other—either positively or negatively. This week, focus on making decisions that have a positive effect on both of you.

PRAYER FOR THE WEEK

Lord, help us to care for each other as we would care for ourselves. Teach us to be thoughtful when we make decisions so that we can live an "interdependent" life together. Help us to avoid self-ish, independent decisions, because we know we have become a new entity—we are now one. Thank you for the love you have taught us to have for each other—a love that helps us find our identity together in you.

Week 5

Better Together

Do nothing out of selfish ambition or vain conceit, but in humility consider others better than yourselves. Each of you should look not only to your own interests, but also the interests of others.

Philippians 2:3–4

Jack's life was going to be a great adventure. He would travel the world, get a taste of just about everything he wanted to see and do—and Jane, the love of his life, would join him in that adventure. It was his dream. But after marrying Jane, he discovered his dream would have been a nightmare for her. Jane's dream was to raise a family in one place that she could call home. Traveling from one country to another was the very last thing she wanted to do with her life.

As it turned out, Jack's dream didn't make much sense if Jane was to be his life partner. His dream had to become their dream. At first, they tried moving around the country a few times, but Jane was miserable. It soon became clear that if Jane were to be happy, they couldn't be world travelers.

Since Jane, not travel, was the most important part of Jack's dream, they had to come up with a new adventure that could make both of them happy. And the one they finally developed turned out to be very different than what Jack had first envisioned. But since it worked for both of them, it became their dream.

Day 1

When you were a child or a teenager, what did you dream you would do in your life? What were your hopes and ambitions? Some fall by the wayside as we grow older, while other dreams may become careers or hobbies. Last week, we introduced the idea of having an interdependent life instead of an independent one. An interdependent life is one that's mutually enjoyable, while an independent life is enjoyable for only one spouse.

The couple you read about in this week's vignette could easily have been named Bill and Joyce—their story mirrors ours. When we were first married, I quickly discovered that the life I was planning to live would have been enjoyable for me but miserable for Joyce. So if we wanted to stay happily married we needed to go back to the drawing board to create a lifestyle that pleased us both. And that's exactly what we did. Forty-eight years later we are still living that lifestyle, as happy as any couple could be. This week we'll show you how to do the same thing.

Your personal dreams in life can be a good starting point for discussion. But the lifestyle that will make you the happiest and most fulfilled may turn out to be something that never occurred to you when you were young. By putting your minds together and thinking of how you can both benefit from the choices you make, you'll create a new dream that will inspire and motivate you as never before.

If you want to work together as a team, supporting and encouraging each other enthusiastically toward accomplishing the goals you've set, those goals must be mutually beneficial. They must be the dream you both share.

Where are you headed in your lives together? Are your lives headed in different directions, guided by separate dreams each of you is still trying to hang on to? Or are you led by the same dream, one you both enthusiastically support?

Day 2

When you and your spouse make decisions that take each other's feelings and interests into account, you provide the kind of care you expected on the day of your wedding. Isn't that true? After all, didn't you assume you'd be consulting with each other on decisions that had to be made? Didn't you expect your lifestyle to be a blending of each other's interests? Of course you did. And what you expected is what you should deliver to each other.

Christians are called to look not only to our own interests, but also to the interests of others (Phil. 2:4). But for married couples, this calling takes on a foundational importance. If you insist on thinking about only what you want and ignore what your spouse wants, you will make massive withdrawals from your spouse's Love Bank. There are few things more damaging to a marriage than one spouse's disregard for the other spouse's feelings and interests. If, however, each time you make a decision you look not only to your own interests but also to the interests of your spouse, you will make steady Love Bank deposits and experience the continuing romantic love that will help keep your marriage vibrant and strong.

Are you looking "not only to your own interests, but also to the interests of [each other]?"

Day 3

What kind of attitude underlies the commitment to look to the interests of others? To put the verse we quoted yesterday in context, Paul instructs in Philippians 2:3–4: "Do nothing out of selfish ambition or vain conceit, but in humility consider others better than yourselves. Each of you should look not only to your own interests, but also to the interests of others."

If you're selfish and focused only on your own ambitions and wants, you're unable to consider your spouse's feelings. In fact, your spouse's wishes become a threat to your own agenda! But if you act in humility, you look not only to your own interests—you look also to the interests of your spouse. And that's when you're able to come up with a plan that is good for both of you.

So what exactly is humility? In this context, it's making sure your spouse's interests are being served, even if it means downplaying your own interests if they are in conflict. Of course, if each of you considers the other person's interests above your own, your care is reciprocal and neither of you should suffer for the sake of the other. You both practice humility as you care for each other.

Peter both challenges and encourages us about this kind of humility: "All of you, clothe yourselves with humility toward one another, because, 'God opposes the proud, but gives grace to the humble'" (1 Pet. 5:5). Rest assured, the Lord's grace will be given to you if you approach every decision you make in marriage with humility toward one another.

Day 4

No doubt you've already noticed in marriage that nobody's perfect. Even though you've tried to be humble, you've occasionally been proud. While you've tried to be thoughtful, you've occasionally been thoughtless. Despite honorable intentions, sometimes your actions are selfish and hurtful.

In an effort to compensate for our weaknesses and imperfections, we're sometimes tempted to do simply whatever our spouse wants us to do. If we've been selfish, doing something that makes us happy at our spouse's expense, we sometimes feel we should make up for it by doing something that makes our spouse happy, regardless of how it makes us feel. That's not going to work. Scripture states very clearly that we are to look "not *only to our own* interests, but also to the interests of others" (Phil. 2:4). In other words, if the two of you are one, the interests of both of you matter, and you need to reach decisions that are mutually acceptable. Makes sense, right? But we take that one step further.

You need to not only agree—but agree *enthusiastically*—to any course of action or decision that affects both of you. In fact, until you reach that kind of mutual agreement on a given decision, we recommend that you do nothing.

Sound crazy?

Interdependence goes against our instincts and culture, so people often think this idea is insane—not to mention impossible—when they first hear it. But follow this rule for a while and you'll find it's the breakthrough you've needed to make your marriage mutually fulfilling. A romantic relationship is impossible to sustain without it.

Mutual thoughtfulness is a key ingredient to any successful marriage. By taking the time to discover and consider each other's interests, you will be on your way to that success.

Day 5

As a Christian couple, you have a third person's interests to consider whenever you make a decision—God, your Creator. If you both begin with prayer when you're trying to come to an enthusiastic agreement, you bring God's interests into the discussion.

But there is one fundamental difference between the way you agree with each other and the way we "agree" with God: the first agreement is made between two imperfect people, and the second is between an imperfect person and the holy, perfect God of the universe. This means that what we are attempting when we agree with God is to think God's thoughts after him, to discern what his "interests" are in a particular situation, and to align ourselves with those interests. According to Proverbs 9:10, "The fear of the LORD is the beginning of wisdom, and knowledge of the Holy One is understanding." The deeper our understanding of God—gleaned through praying, listening to his Word preached, and meditating on Scripture—the deeper our wisdom will be. To fear God is to live in awe and reverence of him—to realize his interests belong at the heart of every decision we make.

If you consider each other's interests, while at the same time seeking God's will for yourselves as a couple, then you'll be able to come to the wisest decisions possible. And those decisions will make massive Love Bank deposits for both of you.

PRAYER FOR THE WEEK

Lord, it is easy to become self-centered in how we structure our time and activities. Please help us to consider your interests first, and then consider each other's interests as we try to make mutually agreeable decisions in our marriage. Help us to order our priorities based on your plan for us as a couple. Let our lives be characterized by the mutual consideration and love you have ordained for all those who trust in you.

Week 6

Who's the Boss?

Each man should give what he has decided in his heart to give, not reluctantly or under compulsion, for God loves a cheerful giver.

2 Corinthians 9:7

When Jon and Leslie were first married, they were deeply in love. They spent most of their free time together in intimate conversation, talking about their future together and how they felt about various options. Each of them had a good sense of what the other wanted and needed. They made decisions that were mutually advantageous, and it seemed to come effortlessly.

But as Jon was advancing in his career, the pressures of his job led them to scrap such bilateral decisions in favor of unilateral ones. Instead of talking through issues with Leslie as they came up and negotiating to reach solutions that were mutually acceptable, Jon started to become a dictator. He decided that he needed to make all the final decisions.

Leslie bowed to Jon's decision making at first, even when it was clearly selfish. She stood by silently as he made friends she did not like or made purchases for himself they could not afford.

But one day she decided not to tolerate Jon's dictatorship any longer. The accumulation of one selfish decision after another had convinced her Jon really didn't care about her interests or feelings. She decided to fight back, and soon there was all-out war every time a new decision needed to be made.

Day 1

Dictators tend to make decisions in their own interest and at the expense of their citizens. The same thing happens in marriage. When one spouse is given the right to dictate all final decisions, the other spouse usually suffers—and their love suffers.

The dictator strategy certainly didn't work for Leslie, so she fought back. Every time they needed to make a new decision, Jon would try to have what he wanted and Leslie would counter with what she wanted. We call that the dueling dictator strategy in marriage. They each cared about nothing but getting their own way. Eventually the stronger and more determined spouse would win the battle—but the losing spouse would already be plotting more carefully for the next battle.

Does that sound like your marriage? We hope not, but many couples do fall into that trap. Instead of finding solutions to problems that have mutual appeal, they fight—and after a fight there's usually a winner and a loser.

Or maybe you no longer fight but have embraced the motto, "Every man for himself!" You each do what you please. We call that the anarchy strategy for marital problem solving.

Remember God's intent for marriage: two becoming one (Gen. 2:24). Marriage should not be a zero-sum game where one spouse's gain is the other's loss. If you've lost sight of this truth, pray that the Lord will help you care for each other simultaneously instead of each selfishly considering your own interests to be more important than those of your spouse.

Day 2

Last week we challenged you to make decisions jointly—working together to find solutions you can both agree to enthusiastically. Instead of using the dictator strategy, the dueling dictator strategy, or the anarchist strategy, you use the democracy strategy to make decisions. We call the rule that guides couples to use this strategy the Policy of Joint Agreement: *Never do anything without an enthusiastic agreement between you and your spouse.*

When you first thought about that strategy, you may have wondered why it wouldn't be enough for you just simply to agree to do something. Why would your agreement require enthusiasm?

The answer comes from 2 Corinthians 9:7: "Each man should give what he has decided in his heart to give, not reluctantly or under compulsion, for God loves a cheerful giver." This passage refers specifically to financial giving, but we think there is a very important principle here that applies to negotiation and decision making in marriage: each spouse should work toward finding a solution to which he or she can agree "cheerfully" (or, we would paraphrase, enthusiastically).

The point is that reluctant or compulsive agreement is just as unsatisfactory in marriage as it is in your relationship to God. In the final analysis, your enthusiastic agreement will stand up over time because it reflects your mutual care for each other. A reluctant or compulsive agreement is weak, and can be easily broken.

Are you agreeing with each other cheerfully, or are you agreeing reluctantly? Ask the Lord to guide you both to make decisions that are mutually advantageous rather than those benefitting only one of you.

Day 3

Ryan and Lisa felt very comfortable asking how the other would feel about various proposals. When Ryan was given an opportunity to coach their son's baseball team, they sat down after dinner one evening and he bounced the idea off of her, completely open to her response. "Lisa, Bob called me and asked if I'd like to coach Justin's team starting next month. How would you feel about that? Do you feel that I'd be taking on too much?"

Lisa was accustomed to hearing these questions, and had asked similar questions of Ryan when she was considering new activities. She thought about it for a moment. "Well," she said, "last time you coached, you got really frustrated with some of the parents. Would you have an assistant to help with some of their complaints? It's not something I feel like taking on myself—like I did last time."

Ryan appreciated Lisa's insights into how some of the responsibilities of coaching would affect him—and her. He'd forgotten about how frustrating that was. "I tell you what," he responded. "I'll ask Bob whether there's an assistant to take on some of that, or a parent volunteer, and then we can talk about it again later."

Does this conversation seem unnatural to you? It may if you're not in the habit of negotiating. But if you want a strong and happy marriage, it's a conversation you should have almost every day. Try following Ryan and Lisa's example with a decision you face as a couple this week.

Day 4

If you're not sure where to start when it comes to negotiation, you're not alone. Few couples possess these skills instinctively. But we have some guidelines that will help you.

First, set some ground rules to make your discussions pleasant and safe for both of you. Since negotiation will generally be needed when there is some conflict to be addressed, there's the risk you'll want something so badly that you slip into making demands, being disrespectful, or even losing your temper. Even if your spouse says something that offends you, don't let yourself fly off the handle. Instead, suggest discussing the issue at a later date, when you are not upset with each other.

Next, be sure to state the conflict from each of your perspectives, and then respect those perspectives. To find a solution you're both enthusiastic about, you must understand each other's position well enough to find something that will make both of you happy. So know your own mind, but also respectfully listen and ask questions to find out what your spouse thinks.

The third step is to take the information you've gathered from each other and brainstorm with abandon. Be creative! Remember that your goal is mutual care. Carry around something that will enable you to record possible solutions, because they will often occur to you suddenly.

Finally, choose a resolution to the conflict that works for both of you. Remember, unless you are enthusiastic about the final solution, you should keep brainstorming.

Try using these four steps to tackle a decision you're facing this week. It may not feel very natural at first, but practice will make perfect. So start practicing today.

Day 5

Some couples are tempted to try the time-honored but flawed approach of compromise, saying, "I'll do it for you this time if you do what I want next time." That approach is flawed because it doesn't lead to a mutually enthusiastic outcome. One of you will always be gaining at the other's expense.

Don't give up on finding a solution that makes both you and your spouse enthusiastic. You may need to come up with a tentative solution at first, where you're both willing to try something to see if it works. In fact, we often find that most of our agreements begin tentatively—we'll try it as long as it really does make us both happy. And we'll go back to the drawing board if we realize it's not working as well as we thought it would.

If you practice the process we've outlined this week whenever a conflict arises in your marriage, you'll become increasingly skilled as negotiators. And you'll find solutions to even the most difficult and complicated issues you face.

The truth is that conflicts in marriage should always be resolved by taking each other's feelings into account. Don't play the power card, forcing your spouse to do something your way. Instead get into the habit of looking not only to your own interests but to the interests of the other as well. In doing so, you will live the life God has intended for you to live.

~𝒟 PRAYER FOR THE WEEK 𝒞~

Lord, we don't want to be dictators, to be fighting all the time, or to give up on working together in our marriage. We want to learn the art of caring for each other's feelings and negotiating to make decisions to which we can both agree cheerfully. We know we need to grow in our understanding of each other if we are to increase our care for each other. Help us to be thoughtful of each other whenever we face a conflict, so that we can fulfill your will for our lives.

Week 7

Getting Radically Honest

The man of integrity walks securely,
but he who takes crooked paths will be found out.

Proverbs 10:9

What Janelle's family lacked in fame and fortune they more than made up for in the way they cared for each other. In fact, their deep concern for each family member was legendary among their friends and acquaintances. So when she brought Brad, her new friend, home for Thanksgiving, he was impressed by their loving and caring way of life.

Janelle's dad had discovered which team Brad enjoyed watching most, and made sure the day was arranged so he could watch it on TV. Her mom had prepared some of his favorite food for their dinner. But their genuine interest in his life, his thoughts, and his struggles was the most impressive to Brad. It brought out in him an unusual willingness to share some of his inner feelings and reactions because he felt completely accepted and valued by

47

Janelle's family. His own family was judgmental and argumentative, so when he was with them he had to put on a good show. But here, he could be himself.

Brad was watching football that afternoon when he overheard Janelle talking with her mom, Brenda, in the kitchen. "But Mom," she was saying, "I don't want to spend all of Christmas here. I really want to meet Brad's sisters, and they are all going to be together right after Christmas." Brad could hear the disappointment in Brenda's voice. "Janelle, we don't have many more Christmases to be all together as a family. Dad and I really want you to be here for at least a week. I know it's a little selfish, but I would really appreciate it if you stayed here at least that long. You could meet Brad's family after the New Year."

Brad cringed. If it were his home, he knew where the conversation would lead—straight into a screaming match. But as he continued to listen, he found himself relaxing. Janelle's tone was calm. "I know how you guys feel. And that's important to me. What if I were to come a few days before Christmas and then leave on the 27th? Would that work out for you? We could do some after-Christmas shopping before I leave." He could almost hear Brenda smiling. "That would work out just fine. Thanks for understanding us."

Disaster averted. Brad marveled at the conversation that had taken place, and wondered, *Why can't my mom and sisters talk like that? Could I ever have a family that sounded like that?*

Day 1

What was the secret to the peace found in Janelle's family? Part of it was the genuine care they had for each other. But there was another very important factor: honesty. Janelle had the privilege of growing up in a home where family members openly and honestly communicated their needs and emotional reactions, and they calmly worked out their problems using that honest communication.

Brad witnessed the value of that honesty as he listened to Janelle and Brenda talk. In his own family, his parents never seemed particularly happy; there always seemed to be trouble brewing beneath the surface. But no one would ever talk about it in a calm and intelligent manner. Bringing up any problem was like walking through a minefield.

Do you live in a minefield with each other, or are you able to openly and honestly talk about your thoughts, feelings, likes, and dislikes? That question will be the focus of our readings this week. As we consider this question, remember this bit of wisdom from Proverbs: "Honesty lives confident and carefree, but Shifty is sure to be exposed" (10:9 Message). Isn't that a great way to think about it? If you are committed to a life of honesty with your spouse, then you can live "confident and carefree." But if you hide feelings, thoughts, likes, dislikes, plans, etc. from your spouse, your true thoughts will eventually be exposed, and you'll feel like you stepped on a landmine. Confident and carefree sounds like a better way to go, doesn't it?

Day 2

You may agree with us that spouses should be honest with each other, but you may wonder how far honesty should go. Are some things best kept to ourselves?

It's been our personal experience, and our observation of thousands of other marriages, that a healthy marriage requires complete honesty. That means revealing to each other as much information about yourself as you know—your thoughts, feelings, habits, likes, dislikes, past history, daily activities, and future plans. We call this rule for a healthy marriage the Policy of Radical Honesty.

We use the word "radical" because there are so many who feel that this definition is unreasonably strict. They think that everyone—including spouses—should be able to keep some secrets to themselves without being considered dishonest. But if a couple wants to be completely integrated, two becoming one, they should reveal every-thing about themselves to each other. Anything less than complete honesty isn't really honesty at all.

You'll notice there are four aspects of honesty covered in this rule: (1) emotional honesty—revealing your emotional reactions, positive and negative, to the events of your life, particularly your spouse's behavior; (2) historical honesty—revealing information about your personal history, especially events that demonstrate personal weak-ness or failure; (3) current honesty—revealing information about the events of your day, with special emphasis on any activities that might affect your spouse; and (4) future honesty—revealing thoughts and plans regarding future activities and objectives. In the next two readings we'll take a closer look at each of those parts of honesty, but for today discuss how you would feel about having a radically honest marriage. Do you already have it? Would you like to have it? If not, why might it be a problem for you?

Day 3

Brad had grown up in a home where it was difficult to express emo-tional reactions, particularly negative ones, until they finally came out in a big fight. Janelle, on the other hand, learned early on that it's okay to communicate her true feelings, even if those feelings are negative.

Emotional honesty enables a couple to make appropriate adjust-ments to each other—and adjustment is what a good marriage is all about. Both of you are growing and changing almost daily, and you must constantly adjust to remain compatible. That's why honest, open communication is essential to a healthy marriage.

Of course, you also shouldn't overlook the expression of positive reactions and feelings. Whenever your spouse makes you feel good, express those feelings clearly and enthusiastically, and your spouse will feel good knowing that his or her care is appreciated.

Historical honesty is also crucial in marriage because it helps spouses understand each other. But you might think, *I can see why it's important to share with my spouse what I'm feeling now, but there are things about my past that would be too upsetting if my spouse knew about them.* Is this how you view embarrassing experiences or serious mistakes in your past?

Your personal history holds significant information about you—information about your strengths and weaknesses. Your mistakes are an important part of your personal story that says something about your habits and character. Revealing them is an essential part of being known for who you really are. But as you reveal the darker parts of your life and heart to your spouse, and as you listen to your spouse's revelations, keep in mind that you each have the privilege of reminding the other of the gospel and of your forgiveness in Christ.

Be honest with each other about what you're feeling today and what you've felt or done in the past. Both are an essential part of your marriage.

Day 4

How completely do you share the details of your activities with your spouse? Even when your activities are innocent, it's extremely important for your spouse to understand what you do with your time. You should know what each of you is doing because almost everything you do will affect each other. That's why current honesty is so crucial in marriage.

By revealing your daily activities to each other, you protect each other from potentially damaging and inappropriate behavior. When you know you'll be telling your spouse what you've been up to, you're far less likely to do anything that would get you into trouble.

Think again of the verse we reflected on earlier this week: "Honesty lives confident and carefree, but Shifty is sure to be exposed" (Prov. 10:9 Message). Imagine the daily freedom of feeling like you have nothing to hide from your spouse. You know you are loved, forgiven, and accepted. That is a gift you can give each other that no one else can give in quite the same way.

But don't stop there. Be honest with each other about future plans as well. Some people believe communicating future plans just gives a spouse the opportunity to shoot them down. They have their sights set on a certain goal and they don't want anything to stand in their way. This may avoid trouble in the present, but eventually the future will arrive and their secret plans will be revealed. And at that point their spouse is hurt by the fact his or her feelings weren't considered in the first place.

Don't hide future plans and goals from each other. To do so undermines your marriage. Eventually, your plans will be exposed. Wouldn't you rather live in freedom and confidence, knowing that you and your spouse are working together toward a mutually acceptable goal? That's the only recipe for success.

Day 5

As this week draws to a close, think about whether your own values and reactions encourage honesty from each other. In other words, do your values and reactions help each other to share the truth or do they discourage each other from revealing the truth? Ask yourselves these questions:

1. If the truth would be terribly upsetting to you today, do you want your spouse to keep it from you until you are more emotionally prepared?
2. Do you keep some aspects of your life secret and do you encourage your spouse to respect your privacy in those areas?
3. Do you have well-defined boundaries that you encourage your spouse not to cross?
4. Do you like to create a certain mystery between you and your spouse?

5. Are there subjects or situations where you would want to avoid radical honesty?

6. Do you ever get demanding, judgmental, or angry when your spouse is honest with you?

If you answered "yes" to the first five questions, your values don't support radical honesty. You may feel that your marriage is better off without honesty in certain situations. But that little crack is all dishonesty needs to find a foothold in your marriage and wreak havoc. The fact is that there are always "reasons" to be dishonest. As soon as you allow one to sneak in, you have headed toward having a dishonest relationship.

If you answered "yes" to the last question, you're actually punishing your spouse's honesty. If your spouse is faced with a fight when truth is revealed, you invite dishonesty. Of course, if your spouse has done something that is very offensive, you can't simply smile and say it's okay as long as your spouse is being truthful. But being demanding, disrespectful, and angry will not solve the problem. Instead, simply express your disappointment, and then encourage your spouse to follow the Policy of Joint Agreement to avoid the offense in the future.

If you give it a little thought, you'll see how the Policy of Radical Honesty and the Policy of Joint Agreement support each other. If you decide to avoid doing anything unless you first enthusiastically agree to it, you'll find it much easier to be radically honest. And if you know you will be radically honest with each other, you'll find it much easier to avoid doing something that would be offensive.

Honesty matters in marriage—and radical honesty is the only kind of honesty that makes sense.

⤳⤳ Prayer for the Week ⤳⤳

Lord, too often we're like Adam and Eve after they sinned, hiding and feeling ashamed. Please help us to live radically honest lives, even as we encourage one another toward being all that you have called us to be. Help us to find safety and rest with each other. Help us to avoid reactions and responses that punish honesty so we can be radically honest with each other and with you. Thank you for our forgiveness through Christ; let us demonstrate that spirit of forgiveness toward one another.

Week 8

Harmful Habits

You, my brothers, were called to be free. But do not use your freedom to indulge the sinful nature; rather, serve one another in love. The entire law is summed up in a single command: "Love your neighbor as yourself." If you keep on biting and devouring each other, watch out or you will be destroyed by each other.

Galatians 5:13–15

By the time Alan and Lucy began marriage counseling, they were barely speaking to each other. At their first session, the counselor met with Lucy first—who sat rigidly in her chair.

"I hate how Alan treats me. He talks to me like I'm a child. If I make the smallest mistake, I know I'm going to hear about it—for weeks! He always complains when I buy things for the house. Last month, I put a few charges on the credit card when I was redoing the twins' room, and you should have heard him when we got the bill. He actually *took away* my credit card! He said I was behaving like an irresponsible teenager. He has *no idea* what it takes to manage this house! He does nothing to help. I have been picking up his socks and shoes and clothes for fifteen years and no matter how many times I ask him, he just won't listen. I've had it!"

Alan wasn't any happier. His sad expression matched his forlorn tone.

"I don't know what went wrong. We used to have so much fun together, but now I never even see Lucy. She has all these book clubs and girls' nights out; she's just never home. She's home with the girls all day, and she says she needs the time off. And I guess she deserves it. But when she's never around, it makes me wonder if she's cheating on me. Last week, she said she was going out to dinner with her sister, but she didn't come home until after midnight! And don't even get me started about church. We'd been going to this one church and I thought we were fine, but then she up and decides to go to her parents' church again. I can't stand it! She got the kids ready and headed out on Sunday, even though she knew there's no way I would go there. She's leading a totally separate life. I'm pretty sure our marriage is over."

Day 1

Clearly, Alan and Lucy no longer make each other happy—they're not meeting each other's emotional needs. Look a little closer, though, and you'll see that their complaints actually focus on something else. They're failing to *avoid* things that make each other unhappy, and that's the primary reason their marriage is at risk.

Even if you and your spouse learn to do what it takes to make each other happy, you'll likely ruin it all if you don't collar some destructive predispositions we all share. We call those predispositions "Love Busters" because they destroy romantic love. If your spouse complains about the way you treat him or her, it's time to confront those Love Busters. Left unchecked, they can have a devastating effect on your relationship.

So, what are these Love Busters? *A Love Buster is any habit that makes your spouse unhappy.* While a single thoughtless act is bad enough, a thoughtless habit is far worse because it's repeated. You'll notice that Alan and Lucy complain about unrelenting *patterns* of behavior: they keep coming, giving them both no hope that they'll ever stop.

At the core of these Love Busters we usually find a lack of empathy—we simply don't feel the pain we inflict on one another. We complain about our spouse's thoughtlessness without any awareness of our own thoughtlessness. So in the week ahead, try a different perspective. Look at your relationship through your spouse's eyes, and make a commitment right now to try to avoid doing anything that usually triggers a complaint from your spouse.

Day 2

In Galatians 5:13–15, we read:

> You, my brothers, were called to be free. But do not use your freedom to indulge the sinful nature; rather, serve one another in love. The entire law is summed up in a single command: "Love your neighbor as yourself." If you keep on biting and devouring each other, watch out or you will be destroyed by each other.

Doesn't "biting and devouring each other" sound exactly like Alan's and Lucy's actions? This Scripture reveals the underlying problem these two face: in a very real way, they believe they are free to do whatever makes themselves happy, even if it's at their spouse's expense.

In Galatians 5, however, we see we must not use our freedom to be selfish. Instead, we are to serve one another in love. Remember Philippians 2? We're not just looking to our own interests—we're also looking out for our spouse's interests.

Are there some areas where you've been enjoying "freedom" at your spouse's expense? Are there times when your spouse suffers because you "indulge the sinful nature"?

In the weeks ahead, we will take a close look at six kinds of habits that destroy romantic love and marriage. But for right now, we simply want you to think about the fact that some of your habits are probably undermining your romantic love for each other, and it's very important to identify them and replace them with habits that build your love.

Day 3

Often, our bad habits seem harmless because we're not the one who feels their impact. In fact, most of our bad habits make us feel good. Some of the spouses I've counseled have said that if their spouses really cared about them, they would stop complaining about these habits since they were so enjoyable. After all, isn't that what love's all about—sacrificing one's own pleasure so someone else can be happy?

Expecting sacrifice from each other means that you're willing to gain at each other's expense. Your own personal enjoyment is so important that you're willing to have your spouse suffer for it. Instead of caring for each other, you're caring only for yourselves.

The marriage where two become one doesn't work this way. Rather, both spouses work together to find win-win solutions to their conflicts. They act in ways that are an advantage to both of them.

Identifying each other's bad habits may seem risky. It may lead to hurt feelings. But if either of you is in the habit of doing something that hurts, or even bothers the other, you'd be wise to identify it and sweep it from your life.

Day 4

Take another look at Galatians 5:13–15 today. What does it mean that you were "called to be free"? If you have trusted Christ for salvation, you have also been filled with his Holy Spirit. And because of this, you have been freed to follow Christ in obedience rather than remaining enslaved by your sins. But the truth is some of us don't pursue that freedom; we wallow in our sin and bad habits. We're aware of some habits and blissfully unaware of others. But those selfish habits may well be undermining your marriage, because your spouse is continually being affected by them.

Notice that this passage does not simply tell us to stop indulging our sinful natures—we are also called to serve one another in love. Part of serving your spouse is protecting him or her from your own selfishness. Think about that for a moment. Are you protecting your spouse from your selfish behaviors? Or are those behaviors destroying your love?

You may already be aware of sinful habits that have been damaging to your spouse. But how do you uncover Love Busters you are unaware of? Encouraging your spouse to reveal them to you is a good place to start.

Ask your spouse to name one of your habits that he or she can't stand. Talk honestly with each other about the effects of this habit. Then ask your spouse for forgiveness and ask the Lord's help as you replace this bad habit with one that is thoughtful.

--- **Day 5** ---

Take some time today to discuss how your habits affect each other. Think of a few that you know have a negative affect but you have resisted changing. You may wish your spouse were less sensitive or more willing to get used to them. But the fact remains: these habits are making Love Bank withdrawals and destroying your romantic love.

Here is the most important question: Are you willing to change your habits in order to avoid hurting your spouse?

If your answer is unclear—you're not sure—ask the Lord for guidance. It's his will that you avoid hurting each other, regardless of how much pleasure you may experience by doing it. But he may have to speak to you through his Spirit to convince you that it's the right thing to do.

If your answer is a clear "yes," you should ask the Lord to help you make the changes that will accommodate each other. Remember: if you are in Christ, you are a "new creation" (1 Cor. 5:17). Out with the old and in with the new! He can help you change your heart through the Good News of his grace, and he can help you change your habits as you walk in obedience with him.

PRAYER FOR THE WEEK

Lord, open our eyes to some of the habits that are undermining our marriage. We ask you for help to make changes if what we are doing is hurting each other. Help us not to use the freedom we have in you to indulge in selfish behavior, but to live freely by loving and serving each other. We do this to honor and glorify you as our creator and ultimate guide in life.

Week 9

My Way or the Highway

Selfish Demands

What causes fights and quarrels among you? Don't they come from your desires that battle within you? You want something but don't get it. . . . You quarrel and fight. You do not have, because you do not ask God. When you ask, you do not receive, because you ask with wrong motives, that you may spend what you get on your pleasures.

James 4:1–3

It had been a long day for Laura. The kids were cranky, the phone had been ringing off the hook, and the house looked like a tornado had come through. As she cleaned up after dinner, the little ones were running wild through the house and her husband, Derrick, was in his usual place—on the couch in front of the TV. Laura clenched her jaw and started fuming to herself as she scrubbed spaghetti sauce off the counter. *He never does anything! He just sits there! I have to do everything around here!* By the time all of the dishes were in the dishwasher, Laura was livid. *At least he could calm the kids down or take them outside or something!* But there he sat, surrounded by a thousand things she saw that needed to be done.

Utterly frustrated, Laura walked up to the TV, turned it off, pointed her finger at Derrick, and said, "I'm giving you a choice. You can finish cleaning the kitchen and straighten the living room, or you can watch the kids, but you are *not* sitting there watching television."

Day 1

Have you ever been in Laura's situation? Maybe you consider her approach to the problem both courageous and wise. By taking control, she saw to it that the job would get done and Derrick would be helping, which is something he should have volunteered to do in the first place. But if you've ever been on the receiving end of such a demand, you know it's not as wise as it seems.

Laura has just cause to feel frustrated. The problem lies in how she communicates her frustration. Instead of going to Derrick with the situation and working with him to discover a good solution, she orders him around. Remember? It's what we've called the dictator strategy—one spouse telling the other what to do.

Do you like to be told what to do? Derek certainly didn't. Instead of seeing Laura's dilemma for what it was, and apologizing for not offering to help, he argued with her. He wanted to finish watching the television show. This started a fight that lasted well into the evening.

Now think for a moment about how you and your spouse ask each other for help. Do you tell each other what to do, as if one of you is a sergeant and the other a private? If so, you're in the habit of making demands. It's an insidious habit that, if left unchecked, can destroy your ability to solve even the simplest problems in your marriage.

Day 2

Even though you probably don't make demands on any other adult, you may assume it's okay to do so in your marriage. That's because you don't see the damage it causes. Even if you know your spouse doesn't like your demands, you may feel it's the best way to communicate your frustration.

James, Christ's brother and disciple, addresses this issue very specifically:

> What causes fights and quarrels among you? Don't they come from your desires that battle within you? You want something but don't get it. . . . You quarrel and fight. You do not have, because you do not ask God. When you ask, you do not receive, because you ask with wrong motives, that you may spend what you get on your pleasures. (James 4:1–3)

Apply this Scripture to marriage. When we want something from our spouse, we quarrel. We fight. But what should we do instead? The advice from James is that we would be a lot better off talking to God about it first.

Have you ever thought about this? God knows what you need and what your spouse needs. Have you ever turned to him first, asking him to help you think a problem through? What a difference that would make, particularly in the heat of the moment!

When was the last time either of you made a selfish demand? With a forgiving spirit, discuss how prayer might have helped you face the problem more effectively.

Day 3

Do you remember Laura's situation from the beginning of this week? She and Derrick had a huge fight, and it all began when Laura started to stew about all the tasks she was doing while her husband watched television. What if, instead of bringing herself to a boil, she had turned to the Lord? *Lord, I know you gave me my family, but I am so frustrated with them! I feel like I have to do everything myself, and it's so hard!*

A prayer like that from the heart may well bring some tears. The Lord hears the cries of his people, and the situation might have unfolded in a variety of ways. Perhaps the Lord would have softened Laura's heart. Perhaps he would have moved Derrick to come help out. Perhaps it would just have given Laura some time to think about what the issues really were, so that she could go to Derrick with a better sense of the problem.

It is very likely that the simple habit of prayer could have headed off Laura's demands and her ensuing fight with her husband. And a sincere prayer can work wonders in your own marriage as well.

When you feel frustrated with your spouse this week, avoid the temptation to make demands. Instead, make a conscious effort to turn to God in prayer and look for his direction.

—— **Day 4** ——

Earlier this week, we looked at James 4 and noted that "You do not have, because you do not ask God" (v. 2). Of course, sometimes we *do* ask God for help with our spouse, but our motives are selfish. In this case, God helps us reevaluate what we want by considering the perspective of others.

Let's go back to our example of Laura and Derrick. Perhaps God is trying to teach Laura that she should have an honest discussion with her husband about the division of household and childcare tasks. If you're asking God to accomplish something on your behalf but it seems he's not listening, you may need to take a good, hard look at your request. Sometimes God doesn't fulfill our selfish requests because he loves us enough to teach us thoughtfulness.

We're not saying that Laura had no cause for frustration. Life is full of frustrating situations. But her choice to make demands of her husband won't work. Instead it will undermine her marriage by making Derrick feel unloved.

Think back over the past few days. What were some of the most frustrating situations you encountered? How did you deal with them? Did you make demands of those around you? Or are you in the habit of turning to God with your frustration? Spend a few moments reflecting on your answers to these questions. Are there any lessons God is trying to teach you through these situations?

Day 5

Some of us think that if we want something, we deserve it. We're entitled to it. Nothing should stand in our way of getting it. And we should definitely speak up and demand what we want. But James challenges this way of thinking. He writes, "If anyone considers himself religious and yet does not keep a tight rein on his tongue, he deceives himself and his religion is worthless" (1:26). Do you keep a tight rein on your tongue, or do you blurt out whatever comes to mind?

This week, we've seen the damage that careless demands can cause to a marriage. As a Christian, you are called to keep a tight rein on your tongue—to think before you speak. You should bring God into the situation by praying first, and then acting on the wisdom he provides.

The next time you find yourself in a frustrating situation, discipline yourself to turn to God first. It may be a twenty-second silent prayer for help. But however you go about it, ask the Lord to give you a perspective that allows you to see your problem through his eyes—and the eyes of your spouse. He can give you the right frame of mind and attitude to talk with your spouse in a way that doesn't destroy your love.

PRAYER FOR THE WEEK

Lord, when we are frustrated, it can be really hard to turn to you rather than demanding what we want of each other. Help us to look to you, and not to take our frustrations out on each other. Please help us to communicate our needs in thoughtful ways. Let us develop the habit of praying to you first, especially when we are angry or frustrated. Help us, Lord.

Week 10

From Demands to Requests

A Better Way to Get What You Need

No temptation has seized you except what is common to man. And God is faithful; he will not let you be tempted beyond what you can bear. But when you are tempted, he will also provide a way out so that you can stand up under it.

1 Corinthians 10:13

Remember Derrick and Laura? Derrick was in the habit of watching television after dinner. That didn't mean he was lazy or even selfish; it was just what he did. When Laura snapped off the television and yelled at him to do something useful, he responded defensively and they had a huge argument.

Derrick never intended to let Laura do everything while he did nothing, but it turned out that way. Most evenings she would do the housework and take care of the children while he watched television without hearing so much as a complaint from her. She actually

66

helped him get into that habit. Then occasionally, when she decided enough was enough, she would order him to help and that would start a fight.

It was reasonable for Derrick to help. But Laura didn't go about asking for that help in the right way. In the end, she not only missed getting the help she desperately desired, but she stirred up an argument that would sabotage their feelings of love.

Day 1

The Scripture for this week encourages us to solve our problems with God's provision in mind:

> No temptation has seized you except what is common to man. And God is faithful; he will not let you be tempted beyond what you can bear. But when you are tempted, he will also provide a way out so that you can stand up under it. (1 Cor. 10:13)

In any given moment, you may experience any number of emotional responses toward your spouse: love, affection, anger, frustration, annoyance, enjoyment. Sometimes it's easy to treat each other with patience and kindness. Sometimes it isn't. And at times when we feel especially frustrated with our spouses, the temptation to make demands is strong. But selfishly ordering each other around is not in God's will for your marriage. And if you have the mind of Christ, you don't have to give in to your temptation to be selfish.

God offers a way out. He can show you how to be thoughtful instead of demanding. And thoughtfulness doesn't just please God— it's also the most effective way to get the help you need from each other. Thoughtfulness communicates what you need while still showing care for your spouse, and that means fewer frustrations in your marriage and greater deposits in each other's Love Banks. Sounds better than arguing, doesn't it? Start this week with a prayer for God to give you a more thoughtful attitude toward each other. We'll spend the rest of this week showing you how thoughtfulness will make it much easier for you to get the help you need from each other.

Day 2

So how do you turn a selfish demand into a thoughtful request? It helps to start with the right mind-set: instead of only considering your own desires, consider your spouse's desires as well. Look for an option that has the enthusiastic agreement of you and your spouse. Since almost every decision you make is going to affect both of you, those decisions should be made together. You should be in the habit of considering how your decisions will affect each other by first asking the question, "How do you feel about what I would like you to do?" That's a thoughtful way to approach a request because it conveys care for your spouse. A selfish approach would be to demand it: "Do this, or else." You give your spouse no right to refuse.

But an even better way to make a thoughtful request is to ask your spouse for help. Instead of asking the question, "How do you feel about what I'd like you to do?" you ask, "How would you feel about helping me with this?" That thoughtful request implies you care for each other. You are concerned about how your spouse feels, but you are also aware that your spouse cares about you and wants to help you.

Try this approach when you need some help today. You will not only both feel much more willing to help, but it will also give you an opportunity to understand the conditions that would make you cheerful helpers.

Day 3

One major problem with selfish demands is that they make our spouses feel cornered. Consider Derrick and Laura's example. Derrick would probably have helped Laura if she had asked for help.

But instead, she made a demand that implied he was shirking his responsibilities. And that's when he started arguing. "I do more in a day than you do in three days. Once in a while, I need to relax," was his immediate response, and from there they were off to the races.

A thoughtful request would be a far more effective way for Laura to get the help she needs. But when Laura asks the question, "Derrick, how would you feel about helping me with the children?" she shouldn't expect him to jump to his feet and start helping her. Instead, he should be able to explain to her conditions that would make him enthusiastically willing to help. By taking a few minutes, or possibly hours, to find a mutually agreeable resolution to their conflict, they would establish a pattern of behavior that would lead to many enjoyable evenings for both of them. Once agreement was reached, it would establish a fair division of household and childcare tasks they would use in the future. From that point on, the conflict would be eliminated.

When you make a thoughtful request of your spouse, you should leave room to negotiate. Be open to discussion and remember to be pleasant, identify the problem from both perspectives, and brainstorm with abandon. In the end, you can choose a win-win solution that will make you both feel loved.

Day 4

Thoughtful requests require a willingness to accept no as an answer, at least temporarily. But when we wait to ask for help until we are already overwhelmed and exhausted, it's difficult to be open to negotiation.

Consider Laura and Derrick's situation again. If Laura expects help only when she's too exhausted to deal with the kids and kitchen duties herself, her husband will not be in the habit of helping her. So she might ask Derrick for help watching the kids each night while she cleans up. Derrick doesn't feel totally comfortable with it, but he's willing to see how it might work. "I can try it," he offered. "I could read them some stories downstairs. Would that help?"

"That would be great," Laura answers, "but even if you just watch TV with them, it would be a big help."

Since Laura's main goal is to have the kids under control while she gets her kitchen back in order, she offers Derrick an alternative that would help him relax while he's enabling her to clean up the kitchen in peace. Later that night she hears Derrick joking with the kids as he reads them their favorite story. As it turns out, he enjoys reading stories to the kids, even after a stressful day at work. Laura and Derrick are working together as a team, developing habits that will help them enjoy predictably happy evenings together.

What situations tend to make you feel the most overwhelmed—and most likely to be tempted to resort to selfish demands instead of thoughtful requests? Remember our reference Scripture for this week. What is the "way out" God has prepared for you? Talk to each other about how you can try to avoid those overwhelming situations, and how you can look to God for a way out when they can't be avoided.

Day 5

As you try to make thoughtful requests instead of selfish demands, let each other know when you've made a mistake. But try not to react defensively when your spouse gives you such feedback. Listen to these wise words from Proverbs 15:32: "He who ignores discipline despises himself, but whoever heeds correction gains understanding." If your spouse offers some correction by pointing out that you've slipped into bossing him or her around, accept the correction. See it as an opportunity to gain understanding about the way you and your spouse interpret what you say to each other. Even if you did not intend your words to be demanding, if they are interpreted that way, they should be changed.

When you convert demands into requests, you are communicating more effectively about what you need. Ultimately you want to receive help without even having to ask. In other words, you want your spouse to form the *habit* of helping you (as you develop the habit of helping your spouse). Demands do not accomplish this. Demands may get the job done for a moment, but they sabotage the future. You are less likely to do in the future what you have been forced to do in the past.

Spend time in prayer today, asking God to bless your marriage with caring communication and thoughtful requests. If you can do that, you will be well on your way to a lifetime of romantic love.

~☞ PRAYER FOR THE WEEK ☜~

Lord, help us to take your way out when we are tempted to sin against each other by making selfish demands. Help us to consider each other's feelings and make a conscious effort to find out how the other person feels about the things we want them to do. Help us not to feel entitled to each other's help, but rather to appreciate the help we receive from each other. Thank you for this marriage you have given us.

Week 11

Everyone's a Critic,
Especially My Spouse

Do not judge, or you too will be judged. For in the same way you judge others, you will be judged, and with the measure you use, it will be measured to you.

Matthew 7:1–2

Jennifer had been raised by parents who worked long hours but never seemed to get ahead, and with five kids there never seemed to be enough money. She promised herself early on that her own life would be different. So when a friend from high school got her a job at her uncle's law firm in Manhattan, Jennifer was on top of the world. She jumped at the chance to start a promising career as a receptionist.

John was a new lawyer fresh out of law school, and he noticed Jennifer her first day on the job. He found her very attractive, and he often made excuses to go by her desk just to say hello. Before long the greetings turned to conversation, and a few weeks later they began having regular lunch dates. Eventually, they fell in love.

It wasn't until they were married that John began to criticize her work. At first, she believed he was just trying to help her improve her skills. But after a few months, it was as if she could do nothing right. Her dream job had become a nightmare, and it was all because of her husband's unrelenting criticism.

Jennifer quit her job to become a full-time homemaker, thinking that it would improve their relationship. But before long, she found that John turned his attention toward criticizing her homemaking skills. After many months of constant disparagement, she was too depressed to get anything accomplished. Though she was once optimistic and hard-working, Jennifer now spent most of her time sleeping and watching television—and wondering how things had gone so wrong between her and John.

Day 1

By the time John brought Jennifer to me for counseling—to try to "fix" her—Jennifer was very depressed. After speaking with her individually, I had John join her for marriage counseling. His desire to "improve" his spouse had nearly ruined their marriage—and his wife.

John had been imposing his way of thinking on Jennifer through lecturing her, ridiculing her ideas, and even threatening her. In other words, he was making disrespectful judgments. He thought he was being compassionate by trying to straighten her out, but instead, he was being abusive toward her.

Whenever I'm faced with one spouse who is being critical of the other, I begin by making two very important observations. First, their criticism is not a very effective way to deal with a problem. Instead of creating an environment that would lead to a resolution, it leads to defensiveness. My second observation is that criticism leads to a loss of love in marriage.

The problems John had identified in Jennifer were actually made worse by his criticism. And the feeling of love she had for him while they were dating had been completely erased. Instead of building her confidence and helping her find ways to express her gifts and creativity, John had all but killed it.

What about you? Do you ever try to "fix" your spouse? How does your spouse react to your effort? Does your spouse find it helpful or hurtful?

Day 2

Jesus gives us a very clear command in Matthew 7:1–2:

> Do not judge, or you too will be judged. For in the same way you judge others, you will be judged, and with the measure you use, it will be measured to you.

Think about that for a moment. When you judge your spouse, you invite the same judgment. When you criticize your spouse, you invite the same criticism. Do you want to live in a critical environment? That is what you are creating through your critical behavior.

Similarly, in the second chapter of James we read,

> Speak and act as those who are going to be judged by the law that gives freedom, because judgment without mercy will be shown to anyone who has not been merciful. Mercy triumphs over judgment. (vv. 12–13)

Who will be judged by the law that gives freedom? It's you, if you are in Christ. At the cross, mercy triumphed over judgment. Christ fulfilled the requirements of the law and secured the mercy of God for those who believe.

Consider how this verse can be applied to your marriage. You trust in the mercy of Christ for your salvation. But if you fail to offer mercy to your spouse, you become a hypocrite who will be judged without mercy yourself. Judgmental criticism has no place in a marriage that seeks to reflect God's grace. Rather, Christian couples should aim to show God's mercy, living out their daily lives with kind words for each other.

Day 3

Judgmental criticisms can quickly destroy a marriage, and if they have infected your marriage, you should work vigilantly to root them out.

And yet, problems you may be having with each other must somehow be addressed. If your needs are not being met, if your spouse is doing something that hurts you, or if decisions are being made that fail to take your interests into account, we highly encourage you to express your negative reactions. Our advice to avoid criticism in marriage doesn't mean that you ignore problems.

It all comes down to how you express a problem. We draw a distinction between a complaint, which simply expresses a negative reaction, and a criticism, which adds a disrespectful judgment to the complaint. For example, if you say, "Honey, it really bothers me when you come late for dinner and don't call," you are expressing your feelings honestly. This is a legitimate complaint that reveals something important about how you are reacting to your spouse's behavior.

But suppose you were to say, "You don't care about me or the kids! Dinner's ruined and it's all your fault." This statement adds judgments to your complaint. It becomes a criticism, and instead of encouraging a resolution to the problem, you're likely to trigger a defensive reaction. The problem won't be resolved as easily, and you will make your spouse feel unloved.

There is nothing wrong with suggesting a change in behavior to your spouse; as long as it's done respectfully. But this does not come naturally. We need to practice being respectful when we are feeling calm and collected. Then, we won't give in to our disrespectful instincts when our spouse does something that upsets us.

So what about you and your spouse? Do you voice complaints, or are you more prone to criticism? Can you easily identify the difference? Talk about it together, practicing respect as you share your perspectives.

Day 4

A few weeks ago we encouraged you to be radically honest with each other. It's not wise to hide the way you feel. And it's essential to the health of your marriage to give each other as much information as you can about how you are feeling and what you are thinking.

But your honest reactions should be expressed without being judgmental. You should complain without being critical.

How have you and your spouse been communicating problems to each other lately? Have you made any disrespectful judgments to each other this past week? Ask each other to reveal them if they have occurred. And don't argue about whether you were disrespectful. If one of you interprets the expression of a problem as a criticism instead of a complaint, that person should explain how it could have been restated to avoid judgment. The other spouse should accept that interpretation at face value, apologize for appearing to be judgmental, and make an effort to avoid criticism in the future.

Pray together that God will help you develop sensitivity to being judgmental toward each other. Ask for forgiveness if anything you have said to each other was interpreted as being disrespectful.

Day 5

Paul reminds us in Galatians 5:

> But the fruit of the Spirit is love, joy, peace, patience, kindness, goodness, faithfulness, gentleness and self-control. Against such things there is no law. Those who belong to Christ Jesus have crucified the sinful nature with its passions and desires. Since we live by the Spirit, let us keep in step with the Spirit. (vv. 22–25)

What a great thought—let's keep in step with the Spirit.

We're reminded of the way our children, when they were small, would try to walk alongside us. We would hold their little hands, and they would keep step with us. God comes alongside us, even with our little steps, and enables us to walk alongside him. And we begin to see the fruit of his presence in our lives—including gentleness and kindness and self-control, some of the characteristics most needed when we have been guilty of making disrespectful judgments. As we rely moment-by-moment on his Holy Spirit for guidance, we will see changes in our behavior.

Remind yourselves that the Holy Spirit is at work in you. Get into the habit of asking the Lord to make you aware of the times when you are tempted to show disrespect and a lack of kindness to your spouse. He will help you overcome your tendency to be critical.

If you have been critical of your spouse in the past, repent of that behavior and ask for your spouse's forgiveness. If your spouse fails to see how he or she criticizes you, bring that problem to your spouse's attention gently, with respect. Don't tolerate disrespectful judgments in your marriage; root them out with thoughtful conversation and Spirit-led honesty.

PRAYER FOR THE WEEK

Father, forgive us for the ways we have been guilty of making disrespectful judgments toward each other. Help us to be kind when we express complaints, and use us to encourage each other to follow the mind of Christ. Let us turn to you in prayer when we face the temptation to be critical, and enable us to keep in step with your Spirit. We want the fruit of your presence in our lives to be evident; please give us lives characterized by your love, joy, peace, patience, kindness, goodness, faithfulness, gentleness, and self-control.

Week 12

The Art of Respectful Persuasion

Two are better than one,
  because they have a good return for their work:
If one falls down,
  his friend can help him up.
But pity the man who falls
  and has no one to help him up!
Also, if two lie down together, they will keep warm.
  But how can one keep warm alone?
Though one may be overpowered,
  two can defend themselves.
A cord of three strands is not quickly broken.

Ecclesiastes 4:9–12

Last week we opened with the story of John and Jennifer, whose love had been nearly destroyed by John's ongoing criticism. In counseling they worked through the issue of disrespectful judgments, and when they returned a year later for a follow-up appointment, the improvement was noticeable. John was attentive to

Jennifer, holding the door as they came into my office. He held her hand as they sat down, and he really seemed to be listening to what she had to say. Jennifer seemed happy and relaxed, and had lost some of the weight she had gained while she was so depressed. After a few moments, she shared their exciting news: they were expecting their first child. Life for them had turned around.

Jennifer explained that once John had stopped being critical of her, she became more relaxed at home. She began to enjoy accomplishing homemaking tasks—especially cooking. He raved about the meals she prepared, and she beamed.

John admitted it had been a struggle for him to stop criticizing Jennifer, but when he realized what he had been doing to her—and their marriage—he took his assignment seriously and overcame his habit of being critical. He dedicated himself to protecting her feelings instead of attacking them. John's regret was clear: "I feel like I've wasted these first few years of our marriage. I had no idea how much I was hurting her."

But there was more to their recovery than John's change from critical to supportive. When Jennifer did something that bothered him, he couldn't simply pretend he approved of what she did. Instead, he learned to be honest with her about his negative reactions in a respectful, uncritical way.

Day 1

We read in 1 Corinthians: "We have not received the spirit of the world but the Spirit who is from God, that we may understand what God has freely given us . . . we have the mind of Christ" (2:12, 16).

If you have received Jesus as your Lord and Savior, you have the mind of Christ. With that special gift, you and your spouse have an amazing opportunity to help each other follow God's leading in your lives. But there are great risks when it comes to pointing out each other's weaknesses. If you express disrespect for your spouse's opinions and ways of doing things, you're unlikely to motivate change. Somehow, you must encourage each other to be what God wants you to be—without sounding critical. Does that sound impossible?

To help couples navigate these tricky waters, we draw a distinction between expressing disrespect and feeling disrespect in marriage. Or to put it another way, we encourage spouses to avoid *saying* disrespectful things to each other, even when they *feel* like being disrespectful. This may sound dishonest at first glance, but when it comes to changing someone's behavior, beliefs, or attitudes, expressing disrespect gets you nowhere. Showing respect doesn't mean you have to agree with your spouse. It simply means you are trying to understand him or her—which is crucial in persuading them to change.

We'll talk more this week about how the art of persuasion can encourage positive changes in your relationship with each other and your walk with God. But for today, start by agreeing that when you want to see changes in each other, you approach the issue with a spirit of respect.

Day 2

In marriage, each partner brings both wisdom and foolishness to the relationship. By respectfully discussing each person's beliefs and values, the couple has an opportunity to create a superior system. As the writer of Ecclesiastes reminds us:

> Two are better than one, because they have a good return for their work: If one falls down, his friend can help him up. But pity the man who falls and has no one to help him up! Also, if two lie down together, they will keep warm. But how can one keep warm alone? Though one may be overpowered, two can defend themselves. A cord of three strands is not quickly broken. (4:9–12)

When you and your spouse put your heads together, you can come up with something far better than what you could have thought of separately. You can help each other. You can support each other. You can defend each other. And with the Lord as your "third strand," you will not be broken.

Remember, enthusiastic agreement should always be your goal. So when it comes to encouraging change in your spouse, it's important to communicate how that change will be mutually beneficial. This approach replaces disrespectful judgments with a caring spirit of *respectful persuasion*. And when you try to convince your spouse that a change is not only good for you, but also for them, you are much more likely to get their support.

Discuss the Ecclesiastes passage with each other today. Have you experienced that "two are better than one" in your relationship? How can respectful persuasion ultimately lead to changes that benefit you both?

Day 3

The art of persuasion can be difficult to master if you've grown accustomed to ordering each other around. Perhaps your relationship has been characterized by demands and disrespectful judgments. Or maybe you don't even consult each other anymore. You may have given up on trying to persuade each other, and you just keep your views to yourselves. If you struggle to interact respectfully when it comes to making decisions, it might be helpful to remember some of the suggestions we've offered in previous weeks.

Remember to make your discussions safe and enjoyable for both of you. Don't pressure the other person to agree with you; instead, you should make each other feel comfortable when you talk.

Express your conflicting opinions to each other with respect and try to understand each other. Can you explain your spouse's opinion as well as you can explain your own? It's vital to acknowledge your spouse's perspective, even if you don't agree with it. That's at the crux of persuasion skills. Showing disrespect for your spouse's opinion gives the impression that you don't understand it and don't want to understand it. But if you show respect for your spouse's opinions and concerns, it gives your own opinion more weight.

What is an area of disagreement you've had in the past? Could you describe each other's opinion about the situation clearly—or have you disregarded each other's perspective? Discuss the issue briefly and ask God to give you each a better understanding of the other's perspective.

Day 4

Respectful persuasion never involves an attack on your spouse's opinions. Remember: you are trying to blend your lives together. So once you truly understand your spouse's perspective, it's time to brainstorm ways to test the value of your differing opinions. You might say, "Even though I don't agree with you, I know you have good reasons for what you are doing (or believing). But I'd appreciate it if you would consider trying something I think would work for both of us."

Maybe your "test" will work well and you'll gain your spouse's enthusiastic agreement. Or perhaps your spouse will propose a test of his or her own. In that case, you can test both approaches for a period of time. Hopefully one of your tests will work, but if the tests fail to persuade either of you, go back to brainstorming or drop the subject.

As you encourage constructive changes in each other, remember your ultimate goals: you want to make each other feel cared for and to resolve conflicts—in that order. We've found that there are many great marriages where conflicts of opinion remain unresolved. After all, you don't have to agree on everything in order to fall in love. But if you are disrespectful and judgmental when a conflict arises, the conflict itself could destroy your love.

Are there conflicts of opinion in your marriage right now? If so, brainstorm some ways to "test" your perspectives this week. And if that fails, ask God to help you respectfully agree to disagree.

—— Day 5 ——

Two heads are better than one. It's especially true when one head is male and the other is female. God created men and women differently, and when we respect those differences, we come to understand how well the advantages of one can complement the advantages of the other.

We often use the analogy of a husband and wife standing back to back looking out into opposite horizons. What they both see is real—but different. If you respect each other's points of view, you will gain a much wider, and more accurate, understanding of the world we live in. But if you are disrespectful because your view is different than your spouse's view, you will miss out on what you can only discover together.

An important element of a romantic relationship is the support and encouragement that lovers show each other. Disrespectful judgments do the opposite, so if they have crept into your marriage, kick them out immediately. Don't give them any opportunity to ruin your love for each other.

Remember, people don't change their minds after being shown disrespect. Instead they go into a defensive mode, making them far less persuadable. On the other hand, respectful discussions will allow you to gain from each other's wisdom, especially when you are both seeking God's perspective.

ᴘʀᴀʏᴇʀ ғᴏʀ ᴛʜᴇ ᴡᴇᴇᴋ

Lord, you have brought us together, and we want to be instruments used by you in each other's lives. But we know we need to listen to each other and learn from each other. We believe two heads are better than one. Help us to understand each other's opinions and to be open to changing our minds. Help us to speak to each other with kindness and respect, and to resolve our conflict in ways that honor you, while caring for each other.

Week 13

Living with a Time Bomb

A fool gives full vent to his anger,
  but a wise man keeps himself under control.
                              Proverbs 29:11

When Jerry first met Ella at a charity function, he was very impressed with her zeal to help the helpless and thought he had met the perfect woman. She always made an effort to look out for other people, especially if they were disabled, neglected, or friendless. After several months of dating, Ella was also impressed by Jerry's thoughtfulness. When he asked her to marry him, she was delighted, and they had a spring wedding.

But after they were married, Jerry noticed that Ella became very agitated when people did not meet her expectations. She was kind to strangers, but seemed increasingly irritated the more she got to know someone. And she was getting to know Jerry very well.

One day, her agitation erupted into a full-blown temper tantrum. She blew up over something Jerry considered insignificant—he had left his shoes in the bathroom and she had tripped over them. Ella lit into him with a fury that shocked him. In a fit of rage, she screamed obscenities at Jerry and threw his shoes against the wall. He could not believe this was the woman he had married. And once the dam burst, Ella seemed to be set off by every little thing. Life with her was like living in a minefield.

—— Day 1 ——

When I was growing up, I lived with parents who had serious anger issues, and I suffered many beatings, especially at the hands of my mother. Learning from my parents, I expressed my own frustration with anger, getting into many physical fights with my peers.

But one day I experienced an epiphany. I was trying to replace the transmission in my car, and it slipped out of my grasp and fell on me. I immediately lost my temper and tried to destroy the transmission and everything else in sight. By the time I calmed down, I had put quite a few dents in the car. I looked around at what I had done, and thought about what had triggered my outburst: I really thought the transmission had deliberately fallen on me, and that the entire car deserved to be punished. It was at that moment I realized that whenever I lost my temper, I became temporarily insane. And if I directed my anger at a person, I was dangerously insane.

Now, as a clinical psychologist, I have an even better understanding of how dangerous angry outbursts are. I've witnessed an instance of anger where, in a fit of rage, one spouse permanently disabled the other. In another case, a spouse murdered the other, not knowing what had come over them. Many of those who have seriously hurt the ones they love had never become physically violent before. They had no idea their anger could be so dangerously unpredictable.

Regardless of how infrequent they are, angry outbursts are a serious threat to your spouse's physical and emotional safety. So begin this week with a heartfelt prayer: ask God to help you protect each other by overcoming angry outbursts.

Day 2

Yesterday, we saw that angry outbursts can result in serious injury to a spouse, but they have other disadvantages as well. One is that they are also terribly ineffective at solving marital problems. Since anger makes people irrational, the problems underlying angry outbursts are often clouded in fear and loathing, preventing a couple from addressing the issue intelligently. When one or both spouses respond to marital problems with anger, the problems simply pile up and get worse. Life becomes miserable for them both.

Scripture has a lot to say about controlling anger. For example, in Proverbs 29:11 we read, "A fool gives full vent to his anger, but a wise man keeps himself under control." Proverbs 16:32 states, "Better a patient man than a warrior, a man who controls his temper than one who takes a city."

But I've tried to control my anger, you might think. *You have no idea what I have to deal with!* That may be true. Your life may be full of frustrations, and you may have great difficulty controlling your anger. But as we think through strategies for controlling anger, we want you to remember this verse:

> No temptation has seized you except what is common to man. And God is faithful; he will not let you be tempted beyond what you can bear. But when you are tempted, he will also provide a way out so that you can stand up under it. (1 Cor. 10:13)

Regardless of how impossible it may seem, you can overcome a tendency to have angry outbursts. If either of you has difficulty controlling your temper, pray together right now that God will help you find victory over this dangerous Love Buster.

Day 3

The first step to overcoming angry outbursts is to recognize that someone or something else isn't the culprit—you cause your own angry outbursts. Remember Ella's outburst over Jerry's shoes? She thought tripping over Jerry's shoes made her lose her temper. But that's not what really happened. She was frustrated Jerry left his shoes where she could trip over them and decided to punish him with an angry outburst. She could have chosen to handle the problem wisely, but instead she became a fool.

It's remarkably simple to overcome angry outbursts once you recognize that they are your own responsibility. When Ella began to see that her angry outbursts were decisions she had made and were not someone else's fault, it pointed her toward a solution. By taking full responsibility for every angry outburst, instead of expecting someone else to change, she was ready to change herself.

Once you have acknowledged responsibility for your angry outbursts, the second step makes sense: identify instances of your angry outbursts and their effects on your spouse. Many people who are destroying their marriages with their anger have no idea they are doing so; they think they are simply expressing their frustration. For the one on the receiving end, however, it can be a frightening display.

How do you handle feelings of anger in your own marriage? Have either of you ever felt threatened by an outburst from the other? Anger can be deceitful, so ask the Lord to open your eyes as you discuss these questions with each other today.

Day 4

By now, we're hoping you and your spouse have had some honest discussion about the negative effects of angry outbursts. But what causes these outbursts to begin with? Angry outbursts are intended to punish our spouse. Most people deceive themselves into seeing it as something else: an expression of creativity or frustration, a cry for help. But it's not. It's punishment, pure and simple.

Ella realized she'd been trying to punish Jerry for letting her down in various ways. She was tired of feeling like she had to take care of everyone else, and Jerry became an easy target. Ella had not revealed her true feelings to Jerry, preferring angry outbursts over honest conversation. As a result, Jerry had no idea what was causing Ella's anger.

Once Ella stopped rationalizing her angry outbursts and saw them for what they were—an attempt to punish Jerry—it became easier to understand how irrational they were. She didn't really want to hurt him—she wanted to care for him and love him. Her anger was undermining her true desire, which was to have a happy marriage.

Like Ella, we all find ways to rationalize our angry outbursts: *I was just being honest; I was tired; my spouse should be able to handle whatever mood I'm in.* In reality, our outbursts reveal an unforgiving spirit that wants to punish our spouse. No wonder such outbursts destroy romantic love!

So what are the issues underlying your own angry outbursts? Ask the Lord today to help you understand why you want to punish your spouse. Then ask him to help you provide protection instead of intimidation.

Day 5

Yesterday we looked at the root cause of our angry outbursts: a desire to punish our spouse. So what does the Bible have to say about this? Consider this passage from Ephesians:

> Like the rest, we were by nature objects of wrath. But because of his great love for us, God, who is rich in mercy, made us alive with Christ even when we were dead in transgressions—it is by grace you have been saved. (2:3–5)

Think about this for a minute: we deserved the wrath of God. We deserved to be punished. But because of his love, God showed us grace and allowed Jesus to take all of our punishment.

Can you see how reflecting on this truth can free you from the need to punish others? When you feel anger rising—no matter how justified it may seem—remember how God chose to handle his own wrath. Instead of punishing us, he spared us because of his love. Shouldn't we extend the same grace to the spouse we love?

Paul went on to tell the Ephesians, "Be kind and compassionate to one another, forgiving each other, just as in Christ God forgave you" (4:32). The Lord has forgiven you. By his saving power you can start forgiving each other instead of punishing your spouse with your anger.

End this week by reflecting on God's grace. Then pray together that he would pour this same forgiving spirit into your marriage.

PRAYER FOR THE WEEK

Lord, please open my eyes to the ways I have been guilty of angry outbursts toward my spouse and others around me. Please forgive me for my anger and for wanting to punish those around me when I feel disappointed, inconvenienced, or frustrated. Help me to take responsibility for my anger, and to turn to you and reflect on your gospel whenever I feel frustrated. Help me to know the freedom I have in you, especially freedom from anger, by living in gratitude for your grace toward me.

Week 14

A Peace-Seeking Solution

Do not be anxious about anything, but in everything, by prayer
and petition, with thanksgiving, present your requests to God.
And the peace of God, which transcends all understanding, will
guard your hearts and your minds in Christ Jesus.

Philippians 4:6–7

Last week we met Jerry and Ella at a low point in their relationship. Ella's angry outbursts had wreaked havoc on their
marriage, leaving them both feeling frustrated and unloved.

Ella had been raised in a family that was very concerned for the
welfare of others, and her parents had careers that gave them an opportunity to express that care. But they didn't understand the risks
their angry outbursts represented to those they cared about most.
Ella made the same mistake she learned from her parents because
no one had explained how dangerous those outbursts were.

Thankfully, after being shown that no one should have to put up
with her angry outbursts, Ella saw the light almost immediately. She

could see her anger was temporary insanity. Why should she want to subject anyone to her insane reactions, especially those she loved and cared about most? From that point on, Ella adopted a zero-tolerance policy toward her angry outbursts, which allowed her and Jerry to rebuild the loving marriage they both desired.

Day 1

So you've agreed to eliminate angry outbursts from your relationship, but *how* do you actually make that work? Last week, we looked at the first three steps: accepting responsibility for your anger, identifying the effects of your anger, and understanding the cause of your anger.

Ella took these initial steps to overcoming her angry outbursts. She acknowledged the fact that no one could *make* her lose her temper—she was completely responsible for her anger. She then started to identify specific instances of her anger and the effect it had on Jerry. She was ashamed of what she had done and said to him. Finally, Ella began to understand the reason for her outbursts: she was using them to punish Jerry, which she knew was wrong.

Have you, like Ella, taken these three initial steps at eliminating angry outbursts from your marriage? Are you committed to mirroring God's grace toward each other instead of using anger as a punishment? How is it going? Are you making progress? Pray for God's guidance as you tackle this ugly Love Buster.

Day 2

If you want to overcome angry outbursts in your marriage, it's important to understand the conditions that make angry outbursts more difficult to control. For some people, these conditions are physical—they lose their tempers when they are tired, hungry, or stressed. Ella, however, realized she was most likely to lash out at Jerry if she had not been honest about her needs and feelings.

Deep down, Ella felt that a married couple should be willing to sacrifice for each other. And she felt like she'd been doing most of the sacrificing. She also believed there was an unspoken understanding between them—if I do this for you, you do that for me. So she was doing things she didn't want to do, expecting Jerry to do things for her that he didn't enjoy—such as going to various cultural events and cleaning up around the house. Of course, Jerry never agreed to this unspoken arrangement, and when he failed to make the expected sacrifices, Ella's disappointment turned into anger.

I brought an entirely new perspective to Ella and Jerry's marriage by encouraging them to resolve their conflicts with enthusiastic agreement. Win-lose alternatives were no longer possible. When she realized they could find solutions that didn't require either of them to sacrifice, Ella stopped expecting sacrifices from Jerry. This mindset made her angry outbursts much easier to control.

How about you? Do you expect your spouse to sacrifice for your benefit because you're willing to sacrifice for your spouse's benefit? Can you see how that expectation can easily lead to frustration and disillusionment? Spend some time today thinking about ways you can care for each other cheerfully. Ask God to help you create a mutually enjoyable life.

Day 3

Sometimes, even when we've eliminated some of the underlying triggers for angry outbursts, we still end up in frustrating situations. What can you do then?

The simple answer is to relax. Frustration usually gets the adrenaline pumping in our bloodstream, but physical relaxation slows you down, making it much easier to avoid a temper tantrum. Relaxation also gives you a more intelligent view of the problem. As you calmly consider the alternatives, you are much more likely to come up with a successful way to handle your frustration than if you let the adrenaline build until you blow up.

In Philippians 4:6–7, we read:

> Do not be anxious about anything, but in everything, by prayer and petition, with thanksgiving, present your requests to God. And the peace of God, which transcends all understanding, will guard your hearts and your minds in Christ Jesus.

So in the face of anxiety and frustration, God would encourage us to pray. Why? Because he is always there to help us put our problems in perspective. And he helps us consider the wisest ways of handling them.

The next time you are in the middle of a difficult situation, take a break to pray. Express your frustration to God first and ask him for peace and wisdom to address the problem. As you build this habit over time, you'll find it becomes a lot easier to deal with frustration intelligently rather than reacting with an angry outburst.

———— Day 4 ————

As you work toward overcoming angry outbursts in your marriage, it's also important to measure your progress. And the person who can most effectively hold you accountable is your spouse, the victim of your angry outbursts.

I challenged Ella and Jerry to document their angry outbursts and review them each week until they were completely eliminated. At first, Ella disagreed with Jerry about what actually constituted an angry outburst. But she finally realized his perspective was much more accurate than hers, because he was the one who was suffering whenever she became angry.

Later, after Ella had completely eliminated her verbal abuse and anger toward Jerry, she explained some of the changes in her thinking. "I know what makes me feel angry. It's thinking that Jerry doesn't really care about me and all he cares about is himself. But if I pray and relax, I stop thinking those thoughts. I realize we all make mistakes, and as Jerry and I learn to make our decisions together, we'll make fewer mistakes." In other words, Ella had learned to discipline her thoughts. She didn't spend time simmering over Jerry's latest mistake; she focused on the progress they were making. She relaxed. She prayed. And her angry outbursts became a thing of the past.

Think about the most recent situation in which you felt frustrated. How did you respond? Did you allow God to quiet your spirit so you could respond rationally, or did you lash out in anger? Ask your spouse for his or her honest opinion. Then spend some time in prayer asking the Lord to help you see your angry reactions for what they are.

Day 5

Selfish demands, disrespectful judgments, and angry outbursts very often blend into each other. Sometimes it's a little difficult to know what a selfish demand, a disrespectful judgment, or an angry outburst is, because in many arguments you have them all at once. And they all work together to chip away at your feelings of love for each other.

These three flawed problem-solving strategies—demands, disrespect, and anger—are all very instinctive and can be seen in most of us when we're just a year old. But just as they're inappropriate for children, and we try to teach children to avoid them, they're certainly inappropriate in marriage. If your parents didn't do a very good job teaching you to avoid demands, disrespect, or anger, for the sake of your marriage you should learn to avoid them now.

Remember this very important principle: *how you treat each other will determine how you feel about each other.* How have you been treating each other lately? Spend some time today discussing how you should be treating each other so that you will continue to feel romantic love for each other. Keep selfish demands, disrespect, and anger out of your relationship. Ask God for the discipline and grace to make it happen.

Father, we know we would be fools to avoid the way of peace you have set before us. It's so easy for us to become angry when we think we've been wronged or our expectations haven't been met. Help us instead to seek your peace through prayer. Thank you for the gift of salvation we have through Christ, through whom we have peace with you. Help us overcome angry outbursts toward each other so that our marriage can honor and glorify you.

Week 15

Living with Lies

A lying tongue hates those it hurts,
  and a flattering mouth works ruin.

Proverbs 26:28

It all began very innocently. Rick and Kelly were on their first date after their engagement. Kelly was telling Rick about some of the details she had nailed down for their wedding when Rick's phone rang.

Rick asked Kelly how she would feel if he were to take the call, and she cheerfully told him it would be okay with her. So he excused himself and motioned to Kelly that he would just be a moment. She sat and watched people as they walked past her window. When Rick came back a half hour later he apologized for the long interruption, and Kelly simply said she had enjoyed a little people-watching. But she wasn't enjoying herself at all. She was deeply offended, and she was holding back tears.

Rick had taken calls before when they were on dates, and it had always bothered her. But she didn't tell him how she felt. Instead, she would encourage him to take the calls. Her mom had taught her that it was important never to nag or complain because men had enough on their minds with work. So she lied about the way she felt about Rick's business calls when they were on dates together.

The wedding came and went—complete with a few long phone calls from important clients on the honeymoon. By the time they had children, Kelly had become very emotionally detached from Rick as her way of protecting herself from things he would do that offended her. She didn't communicate her unhappiness to him because she felt she didn't have the right to complain. So her only defense was to become emotionally withdrawn.

Kelly's emotional withdrawal adversely affected her willingness to make love to Rick, especially after their first child arrived. He felt unfulfilled in their sexual relationship, but tried to understand how tired Kelly was after watching their baby all day. The fact that he wouldn't be home until after 8:00 most evenings made him feel it was unfair to expect her to meet his needs. So when Kelly would occasionally ask if he wanted to make love when they went to bed, he would tell her he was okay with waiting until she was less tired— even though he actually felt very frustrated.

In their own ways, both Rick and Kelly were being dishonest with each other, and it was draining their Love Banks.

Day 1

Sometimes a little dishonesty seems like the best way to love our spouse. "I just want to protect my spouse's feelings," you might argue. But look at Rick and Kelly. They were being dishonest to protect each other's feelings, but their dishonesty ultimately destroyed their feelings of love by leaving important issues unresolved.

Instead of keeping their thoughts and feelings from each other, Rick and Kelly should have been radically honest with each other. We encouraged this approach during week 7, urging you to truthfully reveal your thoughts, feelings, habits, likes, dislikes, past history, daily activities, and future plans. This approach gets marital problems on the table as soon as they arise so you can solve them before they do much damage.

With radical honesty, Rick and Kelly could have understood each other's perspectives and found solutions that strengthened their relationship. Instead, their dishonesty slowly drained away their love. Dishonesty—no matter how well-intentioned—ruins a couple's love for each other. It's a Love Buster that can silently erode your marriage.

Have you and your spouse been radically honest with each other? Or do you sometimes withhold information from each other as a way to protect each other's feelings? Start this week with a renewed commitment to be completely honest with each other.

Day 2

In Proverbs 26 we come across a passage that is very clear on the topic of dishonesty:

> A malicious man disguises himself with his lips,
>   but in his heart he harbors deceit.
> Though his speech is charming, do not believe him,
>   for seven abominations fill his heart.
> His malice may be concealed by deception,
>   but his wickedness will be exposed in the assembly.
> If a man digs a pit, he will fall into it;
>   if a man rolls a stone, it will roll back on him.
> A lying tongue hates those it hurts,
>   and a flattering mouth works ruin. (vv. 24–28)

Do you disguise yourself with your lips, or are your thoughts and feelings clear to your spouse? Do you speak charming words, deceiving those who hear you—even if you tell yourself it's for their benefit?

The writer of Proverbs is clear: "A lying tongue hates those it hurts, and a flattering mouth works ruin." We might think flattery just makes the hearer feel better, but here we find it actually leads to ruin.

But if I tell my spouse the truth, they'll feel bad. Have you ever felt that way? Most married people have. Or you may occasionally turn to lies as a way to make yourself look better. What's even worse, you may lie to avoid getting into trouble with your spouse. You know your spouse wouldn't approve of something you've done, so you deny doing it. While the motives and excuses for dishonesty may vary, the results are always the same: the marriage suffers.

Discuss the Proverbs passage with your spouse today. What kind of "ruin" could dishonesty bring to a marriage?

Day 3

In our opening illustration, Rick and Kelly practiced a very common type of dishonesty when they failed to reveal their true thoughts and feelings: protection. They were trying to protect one another from unpleasant information.

Most of us have lied to protect someone's feelings. But when this happens, we become "protector liars." It may seem innocent at the time—the caring thing to do. But is it? Lying doesn't protect. It *denies* a spouse critical information.

Kelly was "protecting" Rick by lying to him about how offended she felt when his cell phone interruptions and late evenings took priority over her interests. Rick was "protecting" Kelly by lying to her about how much their lovemaking meant to him. He gave her the impression he could take it or leave it, which fed her belief that she didn't mean that much to him.

Because neither one expressed how they really felt, massive withdrawals were being made from both Love Banks—and no one knew. They just pretended nothing was wrong.

Have you been "protecting" your spouse? Are you withholding critical information your spouse really needs to know? It's time to be honest with each other about your feelings. Spend time together in prayer, asking God for help in addressing the issues you need to reveal. Pledge your radical honesty to one another, and make a sincere effort to keep your promise.

Day 4

Sometimes we lie to protect each other's feelings. But another frequent reason for lying in marriage is a desire to look good. Some people need admiration and approval so much that they try to make themselves look better than they actually are—sometimes by embellishing the truth, and sometimes by making things up from scratch.

Another form of dishonesty that creeps into marriage is lying to avoid trouble. Spouses hide information from each other, knowing the other would be disappointed or displeased. This could be a simple lie, such as hiding a small purchase from your spouse. Or these lies may create a complex web that hides a secret life.

We often try to excuse these lies, thinking: *I just want to avoid a big fight, is that so bad?* Or *Is it really such a big deal if I exaggerate a little?* But lies of any form have immensely destructive power. When they are discovered, your spouse will feel betrayed, leaving a huge dent in your relationship.

Do you ever struggle with lying to look good? Does your desire for approval or admiration lead you to embellish your stories and accomplishments? Do you lie to avoid trouble with your spouse and to avoid conflict? If so, confess this dishonesty to the Lord and to your spouse today. Don't allow a "flattering mouth" to work ruin in your marriage by concealing the truth about yourself.

Day 5

Throughout this week, we've seen the various ways lying can creep into marriage and how those lies can damage love. As Christians, we have an added motivation to seek truth in our relationships. We follow Jesus, who is the Way, the *Truth*, and the Life. That truth should be reflected in our marriages.

Have you allowed dishonesty in your own relationship? Look each other in the eye today and ask, "Have you ever lied to me?" If the honest answer is "yes," you've made a very important decision to be honest by revealing the *fact* that you've been dishonest. And you should also reveal the *way* in which you have tended to be dishonest.

You will notice that radical honesty leaves no room for "privacy" in marriage. You can't engage in some kind of secret second life behind your spouse's back if you are committed to radical honesty with each other. Just as God knows everything you are doing and thinking, your spouse should also know. But as you reveal your real self to your spouse, you will not only have a much more passionate and successful marriage, you will also be helping each other become more Christlike.

If you want your love to thrive, you need to know each other better than you know anyone else. Lies undermine this kind of emotional closeness. End this week by asking yourself this question: *Does my spouse really know me?* Ask God to renew a spirit of openness and honesty in your marriage today.

⟶ PRAYER FOR THE WEEK ⟵

It's sometimes easier, Lord, to tell little lies than it is to confront conflict head-on. But we realize that when we withhold critical information from each other, we not only fail to solve our problems, but we also disappoint you. Please give us the courage and humility to be honest with each other and to hear each other's feelings and concerns. Help us to protect our marriage by always telling each other the truth.

Week 16

Uprooting Dishonesty

> Do not lie to each other, since you have taken off your old self with its practices and have put on the new self, which is being renewed in knowledge in the image of its Creator.
>
> Colossians 3:9–10

Alan was a trying-to-look-good liar. When he was dating Laura, he knew she had done well academically, so he made up stories about his own achievements. The truth was that he barely made it through school, and he struggled with motivation. Then, after they were married, Alan exaggerated his achievements at work. His stories were so convincing that he even believed some of them himself. Alan and Laura's entire relationship was built on a web of lies that could unravel at any moment.

Alan was afraid Laura would judge him harshly if she really knew what was going on at work, so he lied about it. After a terrible week, he was told he was being demoted to a sales assistant position. His supervisor told Alan he was giving him one last chance to hold on to a job with the company. Alan told himself that Laura would never understand, and instead told her he had been given a promotion.

But Laura unraveled his web of lies. One day she called his supervisor because his paychecks had not reflected the raise he said he was going to get. She was devastated to hear the truth that he had been demoted and had one last chance to prove he could make it in sales. Alan was caught in his lie, and Laura saw him for the lying underachiever he was. Needless to say, she was deeply hurt; not simply because Alan had been demoted because of his poor performance, but because he had lied about everything. Laura felt like she was married to a stranger.

Day 1

Dishonesty often seems like a harmless way to keep the peace, especially if we are only telling "little" lies. But when any lie is discovered, it makes massive Love Bank withdrawals. The deceived spouse no longer feels safe, cannot trust the lying spouse, and feels terribly betrayed. Lies are often told with sincere-looking eyes, giving little warning that dishonest words are coming from the lips. When a deceived spouse reflects on the effort made by the lying spouse to hide the truth, all trust is lost, and romantic love is lost along with it.

Alan cared about Laura; that's why he wanted so badly for her to admire him. But lying to make himself look good eventually led to even more lies. When he was demoted, he realized he would either have to give up his charade or tell further lies to avoid trouble. In the end, all those lies undermined his real desire for Laura's love and admiration. After discovering his web of deceit, any respect Laura had felt for him was completely destroyed.

Last week we asked you to begin the process of uncovering dishonesty in your own marriage. Are you a protector liar, a trying-to-look-good liar, or an avoid-trouble liar? And what do you tend to lie about: your emotional reactions, your past history, your present activities, or your future plans?

If you haven't done so already, talk with your spouse about the areas of dishonesty that have crept into your marriage. Ask God to bless your efforts at getting rid of them this week.

Day 2

We've already discussed many practical reasons to stop lying to your spouse, even about "little" things in your marriage. But have you considered the most important one? God has commanded us not to lie. It's one of his Ten Commandments (Exod. 20:16). But the apostle Paul expands our understanding of why lying should have no place in our lives:

> Do not lie to each other, since you have taken off your old self with its practices and have put on the new self, which is being renewed in knowledge in the image of its Creator. (Col. 3:9–10)

We already know that lying develops mistrust, creates webs of deception, and destroys marriages in so many other ways. But Paul tells us to avoid lying for another reason—because it's part of the "old man," the person we are without Christ. Now that we are new people, and want to put on the mind of Christ, we should avoid lying. Our God is a God of truth, not of deception. Satan is the deceiver (2 Cor. 11:13–15).

There should be no room in your lives for deceit now that you are in Christ. If your desire is to become like him, then you should practice radical honesty together in humility, rather than trying to hide your weaknesses and living in fear of being discovered.

How has your marriage reflected your "new life" in Christ? Spend some time discussing how honesty will help you conform to the mind of Christ.

Day 3

Hopefully by now you've taken the time to identify areas of dishonesty in your relationship. If you want to root them out completely, here are some steps that can help.

- Describe your dishonesty.
- Describe the conditions that seem to trigger your dishonesty. Include physical setting, people, behavior of others involved, and any other conditions.
- What changes in those conditions would help you avoid dishonesty? And which of those changes would have your spouse's enthusiastic agreement?
- Make a plan, working together, to change these conditions. Include a deadline so you will be able to measure your success.

You'll notice these suggestions are aimed at helping you eliminate the triggers for your dishonesty. Once you remove those triggers, the temptation to be dishonest loses its power almost immediately. For example, maybe there are certain people who encourage you to do things that offend your spouse, and you lie to stay out of trouble. If you give up these relationships, you will have eliminated one of the reasons you've been dishonest. Or perhaps you lie about how you spend your money. You might try keeping your funds in a joint checking account to which you both have online access. Knowing your spouse will see all your purchases will remove your temptation to lie about them.

Whatever your triggers for lying, take some time today to develop a plan for eliminating them. Then commit your plan to the Lord with a time of prayer.

Day 4

In the quest to build honesty into your marriage, it might be helpful to review some of the other Love Busters that we have already discussed:

selfish demands, disrespectful judgments, and angry outbursts. These habits indulge your sinful nature and can destroy your love for each other. But they can also make dishonesty more tempting if honesty is punished by any of these destructive habits. By eliminating them in your marriage, it will be much easier to tell the truth.

Dishonesty also becomes more tempting when couples fail to seek enthusiastic joint agreement in their decisions. If you have done something that you know your spouse would find objectionable, you might be tempted to lie about it in an effort to stay out of trouble. But the lie itself usually creates more offense than the objectionable act. You can remove this common cause of dishonesty by making mutually agreeable decisions. By avoiding activities your spouse finds offensive, there would be much less reason to be dishonest.

Have you been effective at rooting out selfish demands, disrespect, and anger—or could some of these bad habits be making honesty more difficult for you? Are you working together to make decisions you both can live with—or have some one-sided choices been giving you reason to lie?

Day 5

Earlier this week we read Colossians 3:9–10 and saw how dishonesty is part of the "old nature" we had before Christ. So what should our "new nature" look like? The verses that follow offer this insight:

> Therefore, as God's chosen people, holy and dearly loved, clothe yourselves with compassion, kindness, humility, gentleness and patience. Bear with each other and forgive whatever grievances you may have against one another. Forgive as the Lord forgave you. And over all these virtues put on love, which binds them all together in perfect unity. (Col. 3:12–14)

You see, it's not just that we shouldn't lie to our spouses; we should also show compassion, kindness, humility, gentleness, and patience. We forgive each other. We care for each other.

How can we do this? The answer is in verse 12: "Therefore, as God's chosen people, holy and dearly loved." We are part of God's chosen people. We are set apart for his purposes. We are dearly loved. There's no need to hide behind lies, trying to protect ourselves or people around us from our mistakes and weaknesses. Through Christ's forgiveness and love, we are new people, capable of compassion, kindness, humility, gentleness, and patience. And these virtues are bound together by love—love for each other, and love for Christ.

As you work to remove the ugly cloak of dishonesty from your relationship, what kind of "clothes" will you replace it with? Talk about the virtues you'd most like to develop in your relationship with your spouse.

Prayer for the Week

Lord, the good news of your love for us helps give us the courage and humility to be honest. Please open our eyes to the ways we have been dishonest in our marriage and with others. Help us avoid being dishonest to each other, even with "little white lies." Help us to repent when we have offended each other, and help us forgive each other when we've been offended. Being aware of your forgiveness and love for us, we ask you to help us to be compassionate, kind, humble, gentle, and patient with each other. As your chosen people, we do this to glorify you.

Week 17

The Dripping Faucet

Dealing with Annoying Habits

If a man loudly blesses his neighbor early in the morning,
it will be taken as a curse.

Proverbs 27:14

Chelsea sighed with exasperation. "Is it completely impossible for you to pick up after yourself?" She was holding Bob's shoes, sweater, and books that he had dropped on the floor by the front door on his way inside.

Bob looked at her with frustration. "Look. I'm tired. I'll get to it later."

"No, you won't!" Chelsea shot back. "You never get to it, and I'm constantly picking up after you! You're worse than the kids!"

"I'm sorry, Chelsea," Bob said, with a sigh.

"You're not sorry! If you were sorry, you wouldn't do it. You just don't care how I feel!"

But after Chelsea had a chance to cool off, she started to question whether she was being too particular. *Maybe I'm being selfish. It doesn't really take much more effort to pick up after Bob than it does to pick up after the kids,* she thought. So she decided to keep her feelings to herself from now on. Bob's sloppy behavior still annoyed her, but she didn't say anything. Meanwhile, every time he left something out he made withdrawals from her Love Bank account, but remained blissfully unaware of the damage it was causing.

Chelsea wasn't fully aware of what was happening, either. Her feeling of romantic love for Bob was continually decreasing, but she didn't understand the connection between his annoying habits and her loss of love. Every time she tripped over Bob's clothes in the bedroom and his belongings in the hallway, another withdrawal was made. And there were other habits that Chelsea found annoying, such as the way he ate dinner. Phrases he overused. How he slouched in his chair. His gum-chewing habit.

By the time they came to see me for counseling, Chelsea was in withdrawal and wanted separation from Bob. She couldn't explain why—she just said they weren't right for each other. Bob did not intend to upset Chelsea with his annoying habits and she knew it. She felt they were simply his way of doing things. But she also felt she would go crazy unless they split up. For Chelsea, Bob's annoying habits had become proof of their incompatibility.

——— Day 1 ———

Can you relate to Bob and Chelsea's situation? When was the last time your spouse did something that annoyed you? Last week? Yesterday? An hour ago? If you're male, the answer is probably "last week," if at all. If you're female, it's more likely to be, "about a minute ago." For some reason, women seem to find men much more annoying than men find women.

Whether male or female, though, our annoying habits will frustrate our spouse. And even worse, annoying habits can make them feel uncared for and slowly erode their feelings of romantic love. Every time Chelsea picked up after Bob, a little more of her love drained away. Instead of one large conflict or outburst destroying it, Bob and Chelsea's relationship was being chipped away by one little annoying incident after another.

This week, we encourage you to pray that the Lord will open your hearts to hear from each other about your annoying habits without being defensive or angry. You may feel hurt and surprised when you first discover that some things you've been doing for years are annoying to your spouse. You might feel like Chelsea—that annoying habits are evidence of your basic incompatibility.

If you are identified as an "annoying spouse," pray for a spirit of humility this week. Ask God to help you make changes as a way of caring for your spouse and honoring him or her. You'll be able to make your spouse's life much more enjoyable by plugging up that pesky Love Bank leak.

Day 2

In Proverbs 27:14 we read, "If a man loudly blesses his neighbor early in the morning, it will be taken as a curse."

This verse gives a very vivid picture of annoying behavior. Someone is doing something he considers a blessing—the only problem is that it is loud and too early in the morning, so the neighbor experiences it as a curse. This is typical of annoying behavior—you have no idea it's annoying, but it's driving the other person crazy.

Think about your own habits for a moment. Are there things you do that you *know* annoy your spouse? Why do you do them? Most likely, you're not doing them because you want to upset your spouse—you do them because you've never made an effort to change.

Perhaps your spouse, like Chelsea, has not informed you about any annoying habits. But it doesn't mean they aren't there. You may be blissfully unaware of the damage that's being done to your Love Bank account. With a little communication and self-reflection, however, you can discover these habits and rid yourself of these unrelenting sources of irritation.

Changing one's habits requires discipline, but it also requires empathy. This week, spend time in prayer asking the Lord to increase your awareness of how your spouse reacts to your behavior. Try to imagine yourself feeling the same way your spouse feels.

Day 3

Some people might argue that annoying behaviors are no big deal. That's how Bob felt when he first came with Chelsea for counseling. After Chelsea shared some illustrations of what she considered to be their "incompatibility" in our first session, Bob responded by saying, "If Chelsea really loved me, she would accept me for who I am. She wouldn't be so worked up over all of these little things."

Couples often sit in my office and try to convince me they should be able to do whatever they please—that the objecting spouse should adjust to the annoying habits. After all, they're not done to intentionally bother the other person. But if I could swap their minds—Bob becomes Chelsea for a day and feels what she feels when he leaves his stuff everywhere or slouches in his chair—he would understand why he should become more considerate.

Take another look at Philippians 2:3–4:

> Do nothing out of selfish ambition or vain conceit, but in humility consider others better than yourselves. Each of you should look not only to your own interests, but also to the interests of others.

Being considerate of your spouse requires humility and thinking of his or her interests before you do something.

If you are being radically honest with each other, you should share any habits or behaviors that you find annoying. And then, as a way to show care for your spouse, you need to eliminate those annoying habits. As you work through this process, you'll find that you become more compatible—and as a result, you'll increase your love for each other.

Day 4

Intentional or not, our habits affect the way our spouse feels about us. So a couple who wants to stay in love must pay close attention to the way they affect each other. If they ignore that reality, they are very likely to drift out of love. Annoying habits may seem petty or small, but if they aren't addressed, a marriage won't be what either spouse wants it to be.

Because annoying habits usually have an element of innocence, couples don't generally view them with the same seriousness as, say, angry outbursts, which are an intentional effort to hurt the other spouse. And I would agree with that analysis. Angry outbursts are truly a show-stopper when it comes to marriage. You simply cannot solve your problems as long as they exist.

But over the long run, annoying habits might actually drain more love out of a relationship than angry outbursts. That's because annoying habits aren't sporadic—they are unrelenting, day after day, week after week, month after month. If you and your spouse don't consider them seriously, your Love Bank will be like a sieve. Regardless of how much you try to spark the romance, those annoying habits will keep draining the love away.

Take note of your feelings for each other today. Were there any incidents—no matter how minor—that made you feel annoyed with your spouse? Practice honesty by sharing these incidents with your spouse and listening to that feedback with a spirit of humility.

Day 5

If you have committed yourselves to making thoughtful requests instead of selfish demands, to speaking with respectful persuasion rather than disrespectful judgments, to eliminating angry outbursts completely, and to being honest with each other, then overcoming your annoying habits will simply be another step in the process of eliminating obstacles to your love for each other. Remember: your goal in your marriage is to bring the mind of Christ to bear in all of these areas of your life, and to live in humility and love because of what he has already done for you.

So get started today. Begin with a prayer for grace and humility. Then make a list of each other's habits that you find annoying. If one of your lists is much longer than the other, try not to react defensively or with hopelessness. Instead, consider it a necessity in building a more godly marriage.

If you're doing something that bothers your spouse, out of reverence for Christ and love for your spouse, make a commitment to stop doing it. Then, rather than having a home characterized by the annoyance of dripping water, your home will be a sanctuary of peace.

PRAYER FOR THE WEEK

Lord, we haven't given as much thought to our annoying habits as we should. It's been easy for us to fall into the trap of thinking we should put up with these behaviors rather than recognizing how thoughtless they are. Please grant us courage to express habits that annoy us, humility to be able to acknowledge them, and empathy to help overcome them through the self-control that comes from your Holy Spirit. Forgive us for the ways we have sinned against each other, both by what we have done and by what we have left undone. Thank you for loving and forgiving us; help us to extend that love and forgiveness to each other.

Week 18

Fixing the Leak

Overcoming Annoying Habits

For though we live in the world, we do not wage war as the world does. The weapons we fight with are not the weapons of the world. On the contrary, they have divine power to demolish strongholds. We demolish arguments and every pretension that sets itself up against the knowledge of God, and we take captive every thought to make it obedient to Christ.

2 Corinthians 10:3–5

L ast week, we met Bob and Chelsea. Bob's annoying habits had taken a serious toll on their relationship, and Chelsea thought she would go crazy if she continued to live with him. They came to me in a last-ditch effort to save their marriage.

After talking through their situation, we realized Chelsea had been looking at the problem with some mistaken assumptions. Whenever

Chelsea had informed Bob about his habits that irritated her, she had believed only one of two things could happen: he would either stop doing those things because he cared about her, or she would have to learn not to let them affect her. However she soon recognized she could not stop being annoyed at his behavior—whether or not it reflected a lack of care by him. She decided she could no longer tolerate living with him, so separation or even divorce seemed to be the only solution.

It had not occurred to her there was a third alternative—he cared about her, but simply had a bad habit, one that he could learn to change. By forming a new habit of picking up his shoes, he would overcome that annoying habit and most of the others that bothered her.

With some encouragement during counseling, Chelsea made a list of all the behaviors she found annoying and shared it with Bob. One of the items on Chelsea's list was that Bob had recently started waking the children in the morning with a rousing rendition of "Rise and Shine." It made the kids crabbier than usual and she found it highly annoying. Thankfully, this practice hadn't become a habit to Bob yet, and he was quickly able to stop it.

But other behaviors had been going on for a long time. They had become habits that would take planning and time to change, and it would not be easy. Tackling too many at once would likely overwhelm Bob, so instead Chelsea was instructed to select three of Bob's most annoying habits to overcome first. Working together, they could then try to understand how the habits had started and what Bob could do to change them.

With time, practice, and patience, Bob began to overcome the habits that annoyed Chelsea. Once he'd successfully eliminated the three worst habits, he felt optimistic about tackling the others as well. The leak in Chelsea's Love Bank was being closed. She began to feel compatibility was achievable, so she started doing her part to rebuild the love that had been draining away from their marriage.

Day 1

Have you ever thought about your habits? They are behaviors you have repeated so often they have become almost automatic. Some people awake when the alarm goes off, stumble into their gym clothes, and find themselves on the treadmill before they are fully awake. They are in the habit of working out first thing in the morning—there is no question of whether they will go, because this is their habit. Some come home after work, throw their keys in the same place every night, and crash in front of the TV. They don't have to think about it. It's just a habit.

Because habits are so automatic, we don't pay much attention to them. And we also don't pay much attention to the effect they're having on our spouse. But our habits can have a huge impact on our marriages—for good or bad. Some habits make us feel secure and loved. But others can be so annoying they eat away at our Love Bank balances until there's nothing left. Habits don't require much thought, but changing them sure does. So we'll help you think through what's required to replace your irritating habits with new ones that will strengthen your marriage.

Let's start this week by thinking about your habits. What kind of habits do you have that are already strengthening your love? Would you like to build more? Ask God to give you a creative spirit this week as we aim to replace annoying habits with thoughtful habits.

Day 2

Last week, we asked you to identify any annoying habits that may be eroding your love for each other. Most likely, your lists were not of equal length. One wife I counseled required twenty-four single-spaced pages to identify all of her husband's annoying habits. He turned in a blank sheet—none of her habits bothered him. Your lists will not be that different, but one of you, usually the wife, will probably have a list that is much longer than the other's list. When that happens, it's tempting to conclude that the one with the long list is being too sensitive. But I warn couples that the list is simply a way to identify leaks in each other's Love Banks. Your spouse's list gives you valuable information that can help you care for him or her more effectively. So instead of reacting defensively, roll up your sleeves and put your energy into eliminating them one by one.

Of course, changing a single habit is hard enough; a whole list of habits might appear overwhelming. We encourage you to tackle only three items at a time. If you focus your attention on any more than that, you may find that none will be eliminated. And it's wise to start with the most annoying habits first, since they are making the biggest dent to your Love Banks.

Are you ready to start changing the habits that are annoying your spouse? Ask him or her to pick the three behaviors that annoy them the most. And then pray together for the strength and the will to get rid of them.

Day 3

Yesterday you and your spouse identified which of your habits are the most annoying. Now it's time to act. You may find that a few habits can be easily overcome with a simple decision to stop doing them, especially if they are new habits or ones that don't give much gratification. But most habits require more than a simple decision to stop. Much of what we do is automatic because these actions have become longstanding habits.

In order to break these deeply embedded habits, you'll need to understand why each habit formed and what's keeping it there. Here are some questions that might help:

When and why did the habit begin?
Why do you have this habit now?

118

How does this habit make you feel?

Have you ever tried to avoid this habit in the past, and why didn't your effort work?

As you go through these questions together, it will allow you as a couple to understand the background of the behavior and to think through what would make the elimination of your habit more likely. Usually the reasons for the behavior will be trivial. It's generally just something you have repeated enough for it to be a habit.

Trying to understand and eliminate annoying habits can be a bit tedious, but keep your goal in mind: you want to have a marriage in which your home and your relationship are a haven for your spouse. Rather than being as bothersome as dripping water, you can become a place of comfort and care for each other.

─────────── **Day 4** ───────────

We read in 2 Corinthians:

> For though we live in the world, we do not wage war as the world does. The weapons we fight with are not the weapons of the world. On the contrary, they have divine power to demolish strongholds. We demolish arguments and every pretension that sets itself up against the knowledge of God, and we take captive every thought to make it obedient to Christ. (10:3–5)

There are many self-help books designed to help you overcome or create various behaviors. But Paul reminds us in this passage that we are not to wage war as the world does—even against our habits. Why limit yourself to your own willpower when you have God's divine power at work in you?

God gives us his power, and he also gives us a strategy. Verse 5 gives us an extraordinary statement: we take captive every thought to make it obedient to Christ. As you work at eliminating those annoying habits, take your thoughts captive; develop the discipline of thinking about what you're doing and why you're doing it.

Maybe your spouse is annoyed by the way you eat your cereal, and you feel eating breakfast separately would solve the problem. After all, you've been eating that way since you were a child. But if you take your thoughts captive, you will realize that being together for breakfast is an important part of two becoming one in marriage, which is Christ's plan for you. And when two become one, each person learns to accommodate each other's reactions. So by learning a new habit (eating more slowly with smaller bites), you are being obedient to Christ.

Any new behavior feels somewhat uncomfortable at first, because it's not automatic like the behavior it's replacing. But with a little practice, it will become just as natural as your current annoying habit. Being obedient to Christ becomes almost effortless.

What habits are you trying to eliminate today? Ask the Lord to make you mindful of what you are doing so that you keep focused on your goal, realizing you will not only be more thoughtful toward your spouse, but you will also be following the mind of Christ.

Day 5

Getting rid of your annoying habits is a great way to show care for your spouse. But we encourage you to go one step further: as you replace those behaviors, look for new habits that will simultaneously fill up your spouse's Love Bank.

Perhaps you are in the habit of immediately going to your computer when you come home from work and answering email that has been piling up throughout the day. This annoys your spouse, who feels that your email is more important to you than he or she is. It's not that your spouse doesn't want you to answer email. It's that when you come home, you should first reconnect with each other. The email should be addressed later.

So your annoying habit of going to your computer after work could be replaced with a habit of having a cup of coffee with your spouse as soon as you come home, and talking about the day. You eliminate the annoying habit and replace it with a habit that meets the need for intimate conversation. Two birds with one stone.

If you are going to put in the effort to change a habit, why not replace it with something you'll both enjoy? By creating habits that help you accomplish your marital objectives, you will become spouses who are more thoughtful and caring toward each other. That will not only help your marriage, but it will also help you to grow in your relationship with Christ.

Spend some time evaluating your progress today. How have you done at allowing the mind of Christ to help you overcome annoying habits? What thoughtful habits would you like to start building into your marriage instead?

PRAYER FOR THE WEEK

Lord, we are grateful we don't have to be a slave to our habits. We admit changing them seems like a lot of work, but we want to live in a way that brings joy to each other and helps us grow in our relationship with you. Help us to take every thought captive in obedience to you, and to make the changes we need to make to make our marriage happier for both of us. Thank you for your love and the salvation we have in you. Give us humility as we focus on your cross, and renew our thoughts with thoughts that honor you.

Week 19

I Gotta Be Me

Independent Behavior in Marriage

> May the God who gives endurance and encouragement give you a spirit of unity among yourselves as you follow Christ Jesus, so that with one heart and mouth you may glorify the God and Father of our Lord Jesus Christ.
>
> Romans 15:5–6

Marie and Evan made their first counseling appointment after a huge fight. The topic? Evan had suggested it might be good for their family if they took separate vacations that summer. He had two weeks of vacation coming and wanted to take their boys fishing in Montana for those two weeks. "You can take the girls on a shopping trip, or go visit your sister or something," he suggested. Marie was hurt and furious, and accused Evan of wanting to leave her. "This summer it's separate vacations; next thing you'll be wanting is a divorce!"

Evan disagreed, but her conclusions concerned him enough to talk to me about their marriage. During her initial interview, Marie shared that independent behavior had been the rule rather than the exception in their marriage, and the separate vacation issue was only the most recent instance. In the early years of their marriage she had tried to become a part of Evan's life, but he would not include her in most of what he did. He was an accomplished fisherman and preferred fishing by himself or with his buddies on the weekends rather than being with Marie. Marie spent many of her evenings and weekends alone. As their marriage grew, and children came into their lives, his plans rarely included any of them.

Marie had given up trying to join Evan in his various interests. When he took off on a fishing trip, she scheduled a girls' weekend. He took up golf; she joined a gardening class. He had Thursday poker night; she met with her book club every Tuesday. They lived in the same house, but they lived separate lives. By the time their children were in elementary school, there were very few activities that they did as a family, let alone as a couple.

Evan's suggestion that they take their children on separate vacations was consistent with the way their lives had developed. In fact, offering to take the boys fishing could have been seen as a step in the right direction—at least he was showing an interest in some of his children. But the thought of having separate vacations suddenly brought everything into focus for Marie. She saw clearly that if their lives continued on paths taking them further and further apart, their marriage might eventually come to an end.

Day 1

Marriage should be a blending of two lives, where a man and woman work together to live out God's plan for their lives. But when a spouse acts independently, he or she chooses and executes their activities as if the other spouse didn't exist. Independent behavior acts like oil and water, separating spouses and turning the marriage into a relationship of adversity rather than unity.

Whenever one spouse ignores the interests of the other and chooses to behave independently, the other usually reacts with offense: "I have feelings! Don't you care about me?" Since almost everything you do in marriage affects each other, it's no surprise that independent behavior is the single most common cause of arguments in marriage. It makes your spouse feel ignored and unloved, and it should never be tolerated in a godly relationship.

There's a prayer in Romans 15 that we suggest you pray for your marriage:

> May the God who gives endurance and encouragement give you a spirit of unity among yourselves as you follow Christ Jesus, so that with one heart and mouth you may glorify the God and Father of our Lord Jesus Christ. (vv. 5–6)

Reflect on this prayer today. You are taking a journey together—a journey following Christ. Do you want to glorify God "with one heart and mouth"? Then you must be on the same path together. Ask God for his endurance and encouragement as you build a spirit of unity in your marriage.

Day 2

Take another look at Romans 15:5–6 today. According to these verses, your marriage serves a very special purpose: to glorify God *together*. Everything you do and every decision you make affects each other, and it also affects how you glorify God. There is no part of your lives that is irrelevant to each other or to God. So if you want to live out your purpose well, it makes perfect sense to make all of your decisions with each other, and God, in mind.

Independent behavior thwarts a godly marriage. Not only does it damage your feelings of love for each other, but it also prevents you and your spouse from experiencing the spirit of unity God desires. Decisions you make regarding your friends, family, career, time, finances, childrearing, and recreation should all be made with consideration for each other's interests. This kind of thoughtfulness leads to a strong and unified marriage. As you become a team that seeks God's will together, your marriage will bring him glory.

Do you and your spouse journey together through this life in a way that others would describe as having "one heart and mouth"? Does your marriage glorify God? We encourage you to make your lives an expression of love for Christ and unity in the Holy Spirit.

Day 3

Imagine that your life is a house, and each room represents a different role you play in life. Your rooms might include one for friends, another for relatives, and others for your career, leisure activities, children, and church. And then there's one room for each other— your marriage room.

You've both invited each other into your marriage room, but are you free to come and go in all of the others? Or, when it comes to your room for friends, your career room, and your leisure room, do you lock the door to keep your spouse outside?

If any room in your imaginary house is off-limits to your spouse, or if there are rooms where he or she is only welcome to enter on your terms, you are engaging in independent behavior. You are not allowing your spouse to be integrated into every area of your life, and that can seriously damage your marriage.

Take time today to think through the "rooms" in your houses. Are there any areas where your spouse has been excluded? If so, ask for forgiveness and pray together that the Lord would help you build a more unified home.

Day 4

Yesterday we thought about the "rooms" in your marriage and tried to identify places where independent behavior may be damaging your love. As you look for these problem areas, it might be helpful to remember two concepts we studied in previous weeks: radical honesty and mutually enthusiastic agreement. Radical honesty opens the door to every room, and mutually enthusiastic agreement gives both of you an equal vote for every decision made in that room. In other words, those two rules can help give you a spirit of unity.

As Christians, there's another issue for you to consider. Is your life with Christ relegated to one or two rooms in the house, or has he been invited into every room? Are there some rooms where he is standing at the door, knocking (Rev. 3:20)?

Does God affect the decisions you make in every aspect of your lives? As you spend time in prayer together, ask him to show you his will in all of the decisions you make together. Pray that God would grant you and your spouse "a spirit of unity among yourselves as you follow Christ Jesus, so that with one heart and mouth you may glorify the God and Father of our Lord Jesus Christ" (Rom. 15:5–6). God is faithful, and it is his pleasure to answer this prayer.

Day 5

Some spouses, like Evan in our opening example, want lives that are almost totally independent. But independent behavior in most marriages is more subtle, and this Love Buster often flies under the radar. Many believe that their independent choices—about friends, work, leisure time, or even how they pay the bills—are ultimately made for the benefit of their marriage, and should not be interfered with by anyone, not even their spouse. They also mistakenly believe that having a little "space" makes their marriage healthy.

But the truth is that independent behavior usually brings out the worst in their spouse. Instead of having a spouse who is in love with them, they have a spouse who carries deep resentment over their thoughtless decisions. Independent behavior doesn't create a happy marriage—interdependent behavior does.

God encourages interdependence in Ephesians 5:21: "Submit to one another out of reverence for Christ." If you are following Christ, then you are yielding to one another. Or, as we have read before in Philippians 2:4, you are "looking not only to your own interests, but also to the interests of others." If you make decisions that are offensive to your spouse, you are not looking to his or her interests.

What way do you lean in your own marriage—toward independence or interdependence? Are there "rooms" where you've felt your interests are being ignored by your spouse? Share your thoughts together and make a renewed commitment to seek unity.

PRAYER FOR THE WEEK

Father, it's easy for us to get caught up in our own interests and activities and to neglect the interests of our spouse, the one you have given us to care for and encourage. Help us to be radically honest with each other, and to make our decisions together so that our lifestyle glorifies you. Come into every room in our houses, and teach us how to make decisions that honor you. Forgive us for our failures to be thoughtful, and help us to follow the mind of Christ together.

Week 20

Better Together

Overcoming Independent Behavior

> I have given them the glory that you gave me, that they may be
> one as we are one: I in them and you in me. May they be brought
> to complete unity to let the world know that you sent me and
> have loved them even as you have loved me.
>
> John 17:22–23

When Bill's father died, he asked his mother to live with him and his new bride, Elaine. He had mentioned the idea to Elaine once during the wake, but her response was lukewarm at best. They had only been married for seven months, and Elaine didn't think they were ready for an invasion of their privacy. But that didn't stop him from making the offer.

They had a guest room, which had served as Elaine's craft room, and Bill's mom moved in two weeks later. After a few years, she eventually moved into a retirement home, but by then significant damage had been done to their marriage. It wasn't that his mother was a difficult person, it was simply that Bill had made a decision that had an enormous impact on Elaine without her approval—enthusiastic or otherwise. She was very resentful about her loss of privacy and about the way he forced it on her.

As soon as Bill ignored Elaine's reservations and moved his mother into their apartment, Elaine started feeling resentful about his heavy-handed approach. That resentment grew throughout his mother's visit, and whenever they had a problem, she would remember how he forced her to live with his mother. Even after his mother left for the retirement home, Elaine remembered how upset she had been during those early years of marriage. Whenever his independent decision crossed her mind, Love Bank withdrawals were made again and again. It drained his account in her Love Bank.

Day 1

In marriage, two become one. Or at least that was the way God intended it to be (Gen. 2:24). In these marriages, spouses make decisions with each other's interests in mind, "looking not only to your own interests, but also to the interests of others" (Phil. 2:4). We call the behavior that comes from this thoughtful way of making decisions *interdependent* behavior.

But in some marriages, two remain two because they plan and execute their activities as if the other spouse didn't exist. This was the approach Bill took when he unilaterally decided to let his mother move into their home. His decision was an example of independent behavior that almost always leads to resentment, which Elaine felt long after his decision was made.

We call independent behavior a Love Buster because that's what it does—it destroys romantic love. Whenever an independent decision is made by one spouse it usually hurts the other spouse. But independent behavior does something even more insidious—it helps create an incompatible lifestyle. When spouses get into the habit of ignoring each other's interests, they grow further and further apart until they have little in common.

Regardless of how incompatible a couple has become as a result of independent behavior, compatibility can be restored and romantic love along with it. All that's required is to follow God's will for marriage: to make interdependent decisions. Thoughtless behavior must be abandoned and thoughtful behavior must replace it.

What kind of marriage have you had? Have you practiced interdependence right up to this very day—or have you let independent decisions creep into your lives? Even the strongest marriages can suffer from occasional lapses of independent behavior from time to time. Take some time to examine the way you make decisions and commit yourselves to building greater interdependence in the week ahead.

—— Day 2 ——

The Policy of Joint Agreement (never do anything without an enthusiastic agreement between you and your spouse) is an excellent "metal detector" that spouses can use to find instances of independent behavior. As they go through their weekly schedule together, they can examine each activity to see if they are both enthusiastic about having it there. If there is reluctance from either spouse, that activity should become a target for change.

But coming to a mutually enthusiastic agreement about every decision isn't easy. When a solution is not found right away, a couple is tempted to take shortcuts. They agree to let one spouse do it his or her way one time, and give the other spouse the right to decide the next time. Or it's agreed that one spouse makes all of the decisions while the other tries to live with them. But both of those approaches to marital problem solving are flawed because the elements of their lifestyle are created to benefit one spouse at the expense of the other. That's not real unity.

We challenge you to achieve the goal of mutual enthusiasm in all of your decision making; this will require you to stretch your minds.

At first, it may seem as if you've hit gridlock. There won't seem to be a way to get beyond the "never do anything" part of the Policy of Joint Agreement. But as you respectfully discover each other's wisdom and understand each other's interests, you will start to find solutions you didn't think were there.

Discuss your weekly schedules today. Are you both enthusiastic about the way you have planned your activities? If not, pick one activity that is a problem for one of you and brainstorm some alternatives to it.

Day 3

As you eliminate independent behavior from your marriage, consider this prayer of Jesus:

> I have given them the glory that you gave me, that they may be one as we are one: I in them and you in me. May they be brought to complete unity to let the world know that you sent me and have loved them even as you have loved me. (John 17:22–23)

Jesus was praying for all of his believers, but we think that this passage has particular significance for your marriage as a Christian couple. In this passage, Christ prays his people will be one—with the same unity that unites the Father, Son, and Spirit. He prays we will be brought to "complete unity" for a very special purpose: "to let the world know that you sent me and have loved them even as you have loved me."

Have you ever thought about the fact that unity in your marriage can show the world the power of the gospel? A Christian marriage is an analogy of Christ and the church (Eph. 5:21–33). When a husband and wife live in unity, showing genuine love and care for each other in both major and minor decisions, they are demonstrating the kind of unity God desires. That's why marriage is sacred. It gives the world a picture of how God wants to interact with his people.

Spend time in prayer today, asking God to make your marriage a better reflection of his great, unselfish love.

Day 4

God wants us to be integrated in our marriages in the same way we are unified with him now and throughout eternity. But what does that kind of interdependence look like, practically speaking? How can you actually make mutually enthusiastic decisions when you are two very different people?

It helps to remember the negotiating guidelines we discussed a few weeks ago. First, decisions should be made through safe and pleasant discussions. If your negative emotions start getting the best of you, postpone the discussion. Second, always try to look at the decision through your spouse's eyes. You won't make a good decision until you truly understand his or her perspective. Third, give yourselves time to brainstorm. It may take days to find a decision you're both excited about, so be patient. Finally, make sure the decision you settle on has genuine support from you both.

The way you go about trying to resolve conflict is often more important to the success of your marriage than the resolution itself. If you offend each other in an argument you will have damaged your relationship, even if you eventually find a resolution. On the other hand, if you discuss an issue respectfully, you show love and care for each other, even if you don't find a resolution and end up agreeing to do nothing.

People from a wide variety of backgrounds, perspectives, and opinions find unity in Christ. So let the unity of Christ permeate your marriage, especially in areas of conflict. As you practice making mutually beneficial decisions, remember your overarching goal: submit to one another out of reverence for Christ (Eph. 5:21).

Day 5

All week long we've been encouraging you to build a more unified lifestyle in your marriage. Perhaps you've already noticed that when you decide to become interdependent, you do not have fewer conflicts—you have more of them. At least there seem to be more, because you will address each of them as they arise. And you will begin to welcome them, because they will make your bond deeper and your marriage stronger.

We'll use our own marriage as an example. We have at least one conflict every hour we're together. And yet we have a terrific marriage. That's because it's not conflicts that make a marriage miserable—marriages fail because couples don't know how to negotiate when conflicts arise. Since we know how to handle conflicts the right way, they don't put a wedge between us.

Unfortunately, many couples try to avoid their differences by indulging in independent behavior. This strategy gives a false sense of peace because it ultimately pulls you in opposite directions and leaves you both feeling distant and uncared for. It's far better to face those differences head-on and find interdependent solutions that make you both feel loved.

Since it's so important to resolve conflicts the right way in marriage, we'll take the next four weeks to examine how to handle the most common conflicts couples face. But for today, consider this: conflict doesn't have to undermine your unity with each other or with Christ. Instead, it offers you an opportunity to grow in your personal and spiritual understanding.

PRAYER FOR THE WEEK

Lord, we want the unity you desire for us to be evident in our marriage. Let us have unity so that others may also know who you are. Help us to have the courage and humility to be completely honest with each other and the endurance to work toward solutions that benefit both of us. Thank you for the unity of your Spirit, which inspires us to create unity with each other.

Week 21

Finding a Way through Family Feuds

Finally, all of you, live in harmony with one another; be sympathetic, love as brothers, be compassionate and humble.

1 Peter 3:8

Luke came from a large, tight-knit family. His wife, Amy, had only one sister who was several years older. For Amy, family vacations usually involved something different each year—a cruise one year, a trip to the beach the next. But each vacation was relaxing, with each member of the family reading books and playing occasional card games with each other. Luke, on the other hand, had gone to the same lake for the summer year after year, spending two weeks in a rustic cabin teeming with brothers, sisters, cousins, aunts, and uncles. It was anything but relaxing.

The summer after Luke and Amy were married, they went with the rest of Luke's family to the lake. Luke and Amy shared a mattress on the floor, with several younger cousins occupying the bunk beds in the room. Amy was incredibly uncomfortable. She didn't like other people walking around as she lay in bed with her husband, and the flat mattress and dust didn't help. The family was loud and rambunctious, and everyone participated in unending games and activities. Amy was expected to help in the kitchen, but she felt woefully unprepared under the watchful eye of Luke's grandmother. By the end of the week, Amy was completely exhausted and vowed never to return.

After nearly a year of cajoling by Luke's mom, Luke told Amy that if she cared about family life, she really needed to join his family at the lake that summer. She gave in and agreed to go the second year, and then the third. Nothing had improved; if anything, the introduction of Luke's opinionated new brother-in-law had made things even worse. So Luke unilaterally decided to go on the family vacation by himself the fourth year. That made Amy feel even worse. Even after the vacation was over and Luke returned, Amy continued to feel bad. Every time she thought about Luke's decision, and how he failed to take her feelings into account, she felt megadoses of resentment that put their marriage on very rocky ground.

Day 1

Conflicts that are not resolved the right way can lead to years of unrelenting resentment. When one spouse "takes charge" and makes decisions—like Luke's decision to attend the family vacation alone—the other spouse can remember that thoughtless event years later, and bring it up from time to time. And each time it's remembered, Love Bank withdrawals are made. Think about this type of resentment as "type A" resentment. This is the type of resentment Amy felt, and it happens when spouses fail to follow the Policy of Joint Agreement.

But even when couples *do* try to make mutually enthusiastic decisions, resentment can be created when one of the spouses must do nothing because an agreement has not been reached. You have your heart set on something, but your spouse won't agree to it. You'll feel some resentment every time that happens, and it will be accompanied by some Love Bank withdrawals. Think of this as "type B" resentment. It's the resentment Luke would have felt if Amy had said, "No family vacations!"

So if following the Policy of Joint Agreement causes resentment, and violating it also causes resentment, what difference does it make whether you follow it or not? Actually, it makes a great deal of difference. Type B resentment remains only for as long as it takes to reach an enthusiastic agreement. Type A resentment, on the other hand, can remain for the rest of a couple's lives together.

During your devotional time in the weeks ahead, we will help you manage conflicts that are common in marriage, starting this week with conflicts over family and friends. And we'll help you do it in a way that avoids long-term resentment.

Day 2

Have you ever been in Luke's and Amy's shoes, disagreeing over how you spend time with family and friends? Maybe your spouse can't tolerate spending time with your family. Or perhaps you have a friend who simply drives your spouse up the wall. Some couples disagree over family vacation plans, a place of worship, or expectations surrounding participation in family traditions. Whatever it is, issues concerning your family and friends can become a major source of conflict in marriage.

When a conflict arises between spouses concerning friends and family, emotions often run high. It's easy to blow things out of proportion. It's also easy to fall into one of two traps. You might try the dictator strategy, moving from selfish demands (You're having dinner with my parents whether you like it or not!) to disrespectful judgments (You have no concept of what it means to be a family!) to angry outbursts. As we've noted in previous weeks, this strategy doesn't usually resolve the conflict, and it destroys romantic love.

But equally useless and damaging is the anarchy strategy that results in independent behavior (If you don't enjoy hanging out with my parents, I'll have dinner with them by myself). This strategy undermines your unity as a couple because it ignores your spouse's interests and feelings.

Think of a conflict you had over friends and relatives in the past. Did you use the dictator strategy (demands, disrespectful judgments, angry outbursts) or the anarchy strategy (independent behavior) to resolve it? If so, apologize to your spouse and ask for forgiveness. Acknowledge that these strategies diminish your unity and love for each other, and pledge to change your strategy to one of sympathy, compassion, and humility.

Day 3

So what insight does the Bible offer when it comes to conflicts over friends and family? Reflect on 1 Peter 3:8: "Finally, all of you, live in harmony with one another; be sympathetic, love as brothers, be compassionate and humble." Apply this command to your marriage: in harmony with each other, be sympathetic, compassionate, and humble. Love like the best of brothers, in every situation. If you were both to resolve conflicts in this way, think how it would benefit your marriage.

Your relationships with friends and family are important to you; we know how difficult it can be to reconcile their interests with those of your spouse. But if you belong to Christ and have his Holy Spirit at work in you and in your marriage, you are not left to your own devices when it comes to resolving these conflicts. Through his Spirit of compassion and humility, he can help you to be in the right frame of mind to have a helpful, productive conversation with your spouse as you work through your disagreement.

As you approach a conflict, always begin with prayer—even a silent prayer in your own heart. Ask the Lord to cultivate a humble heart within you, with true love and compassion toward your spouse and the people he or she cherishes.

Day 4

Yesterday we reflected on 1 Peter 3:8 and we encouraged you to develop an attitude of humility, compassion, and sympathy. Can you see how this frame of mind could help you settle conflicts with your spouse? Sympathy helps you understand your spouse's explanation of his or her feelings. Humility helps you consider your spouse's interests to be as important as your own. And compassion leads you to brainstorming a solution both you and your spouse can enjoy.

Remember Luke and Amy's dilemma with family vacations? How could they have applied this biblical mind-set to their problem?

As soon as the conflict over the family vacation was identified, Luke and Amy could have prayed together, asking God to make their discussion pleasant and safe. Luke could have then explained that he wanted a week at the lake every summer with his family. After listening with empathy, Amy could have then shared her honest feelings, explaining that being with so many people was overwhelming to her and she was feeling judged by his grandmother when she tried to help out.

Once they understood each other's perspectives, Amy and Luke could have brainstormed some better options. Could they stay in a local hotel or rent their own cabin nearby? Should they begin their own family tradition?

With a spirit of humility and sympathy for each other, Amy and Luke's discussion would have actually strengthened their marriage. It might have taken some trial and error, and Luke may have felt some "type B" resentment in the short term. But eventually they would have found a solution that pleased them both and avoided Amy's "type A" long-term resentment.

Are you facing any conflicts over friends and family right now? Ask God to give you a 1 Peter 3:8 mind-set, then have a safe discussion and see if you can brainstorm some solutions of your own.

Day 5

We know that your friends and family are important to each of you. At first, it will probably take some time for you to resolve these conflicts the right way. And the longer it takes, the more pronounced "type B" resentment will be for you. But with practice, you can find solutions both of you agree with. And that will eliminate the "type A" resentment that can plague a marriage indefinitely.

So as you end this week, we encourage you to discuss some hypothetical situations: a husband who finds one of his wife's old friends extremely annoying; and a wife who has been attending her parents' church to please them, neglecting her husband's need to go to a different church. You can think of other possible conflicts a couple might have with friends and family. But we recommend that you begin with imaginary conflicts. We want you to first practice negotiating issues that are not emotionally charged for you.

As you negotiate these hypothetical situations, remember to use the skills we've talked about in previous chapters. Make the discussions pleasant and safe. Introduce what each of you wants, and listen carefully for your spouse's perspective of the issue. Brainstorm possible solutions. And finally, make a decision that has enthusiastic agreement from both of you.

As you do these practice negotiations, you'll be building a great biblical habit: looking not only to your own interests but also to those of your spouse (Phil. 2:4). And the next time a real-life conflict arises over family and friends, you'll be ready to tackle it with grace.

PRAYER FOR THE WEEK

Lord, we're often tempted to try to fulfill the needs and expectations of our friends and family members at the expense of each other. When we face conflicts regarding these people, help us to be honest, but also respectful, about our opinions and feelings.

Also, please help us discover the resolutions to conflicts that we will agree to enthusiastically. We want to live in harmony with each other, filled with empathy, compassion, and humility, as we demonstrate our care for each other. Help us to look not only to our own interests but also to the interests of each other.

Week 22

Working Too Hard?

"For I know the plans I have for you," declares the LORD, "plans to prosper you and not to harm you, plans to give you hope and a future."

Jeremiah 29:11

When Josh and Rachel met in graduate school, they were full of excitement about their future careers. Josh was in law school preparing to be a defense attorney; Rachel was pursuing a master's degree in journalism and already had a job as a reporter for a local paper. They married while still in school, lived in a tiny apartment, drove an old car, and loved every minute of it.

After Josh passed his bar exam, he was offered a position at a local firm. He jumped at the opportunity, and put every ounce of his energy into becoming their best attorney. In addition to her job as a reporter, Rachel also started an independent writing career, publishing several magazine articles and working on a book project. After the birth of their first child, Rachel continued to pursue all of her writing responsibilities while Josh moved full steam ahead with his career.

After their second child arrived, Josh felt that if he was going to be successful, he should move to a more prestigious law firm. When that opportunity arose in Los Angeles, over 1,000 miles away, he jumped at it. Rachel was hesitant. They had great childcare lined up, and a move would disrupt her writing connections. While the extra money would be helpful, she was worried about the impact it would have on her writing career and their new family. Rachel expressed her concerns, but Josh insisted it would be the best thing they could do. Rachel agreed reluctantly, and they moved to Los Angeles.

After their move, Rachel was unable to find a new job as a reporter, but Josh's increased income more than compensated for the loss of her salary. So she was able to spend more time with her children, something she had missed before the move. And yet, after a year of living in their new home, she was convinced they had made a huge mistake. She rarely saw Josh; the demands of his job were overwhelming. The children didn't see much of their daddy, either.

Josh promised that once he became a partner, he would have more flexibility, but Rachel seriously doubted that would ever happen. He was now married to his job. She was beginning to resent the career decision Josh had made. She wanted a partner in life, not a paycheck, and she began to think she would be better off with someone else.

Day 1

Josh made career decisions that failed to take his wife's interests and feelings into account, and his independent behavior took a sharp toll on their marriage. But Rachel also made a mistake: she wasn't completely honest with Josh about how much she resented his decision. The resentment just kept building as his account in her Love Bank kept falling.

Would it have helped if she had demanded a change in his schedule to include his family? What if she had been disrespectful, telling him that he was a poor excuse for a husband and father? If she had lost her temper, would that have helped them deal with the problem? No. It would have made matters worse. But if Rachel had addressed her growing resentment in an honest but thoughtful way, she might have been able to persuade Josh to change his schedule to keep their marriage from falling apart.

There are few decisions you will make in life that will have a bigger impact on your marriage than your choice of career. That's because the demands of many careers greatly limit a couple's ability to manage their weekly schedules with mutually enthusiastic agreement. The career takes control of their schedule, and leaves at least one spouse feeling very resentful.

Furthermore, if a career prevents a couple from meeting each other's important emotional needs by making their fifteen hours of undivided attention essentially impossible to find, the career prevents marital fulfillment. If your job requires extensive travel, taking you away from each other, how can you expect to meet each other's needs? We have noticed that certain careers are associated with very high divorce rates simply because they greatly limit a couple's ability to care for each other.

If you want to be in love and stay in love, you must avoid the mistake of letting a career interfere with your ability to come to an agreement regarding your schedule. So this week, we'll encourage you to get on the same page when it comes to your work and time management. Spend some time in prayer today. Ask God to give you wisdom and grace as you discuss your careers and how they affect your weekly schedules during the days ahead.

Day 2

We have a question for you: Would God call you to devote yourself to your career at the expense of your marriage? As you reflect on that question, consider Jeremiah 29:11: "'For I know the plans I have for you,' declares the LORD, 'plans to prosper you and not to harm you, plans to give you hope and a future.'"

Would a career that prevents you from meeting your spouse's emotional needs harm your spouse? What if the career took you away from your children—would it harm them? And if the career harmed your spouse and your children, would it harm you? Would it give you hope and a future?

According to Jeremiah 29:11, God's plan for you will not harm you or your family. Rather, it will give you hope and a future. That plan involves achieving specific goals each day, as we read in Ephesians: "For we are God's workmanship, created in Christ Jesus to do good works, which God prepared in advance for us to do" (2:10). You are God's "workmanship," a work of art that has a mission in life prepared in advance by God. An important aspect of that mission is caring for each other and the children God has given you. The career you've chosen should help you achieve that mission, not thwart your efforts.

Do you think your current careers, schedule, and lifestyle allow you to fulfill God's plans for you? Are they giving your marriage "hope and a future," or have they been undermining your love? Discuss and pray about these questions today.

Day 3

When we were first married, neither of us had chosen a career. So we had the opportunity to discuss career possibilities with each other until we found careers that took each other's interests and feelings into account. Several initial suggestions were vetoed until we agreed enthusiastically on the careers we ultimately chose.

We were very young when we married, so we had the advantage of picking careers together. But today, most couples marry when their careers have already been established. When you were married, you may have already made your career decisions. Maybe you married your spouse in spite of his or her career.

But even couples like us, who deliberately choose careers that are mutually agreeable, can be thrown a curveball after children arrive. That's what happened to Josh and Rachel. Their career choices would have worked out much better if they had not had children. It was their children who required a radical change in their schedules—a change that Josh and Rachel didn't think would be possible.

Regardless of how you arrived at the career you've chosen, and the schedule it demands, we want you to consider the impact it is having on your marriage. If your marriage is part of the good work God has for you, does your career leave adequate time for it? We'll take a close look at that question tomorrow. But for today, pray together and ask the Lord to reveal ways that your careers are hindering or hurting your marriage. Ask for a spirit of humility, patience, compassion, and sympathy. God has a good plan for both your marriage and your careers. Ask him to help you see it.

Day 4

When it comes to time management and marriage, one of the biggest reasons spouses lose their love for each other is that they don't schedule enough time to meet each other's emotional needs. Careers can be a major culprit when it comes to not having enough time together. But other things can also eat up the time you should be spending with each other, including children, church commitments, or family and friends.

Yesterday, we asked you to think about this question: Does your career leave adequate time for your marriage? Today we'd like you to expand that question to include anything else that keeps you from caring for each other.

Do you write out your schedules each week? Is your time for undivided attention included on your schedule? And finally, are you in enthusiastic agreement regarding what each of you does during the week? If you find yourselves in conflict over any aspect of time management, we encourage you to use your negotiating skills to find ways to come to an agreement.

Think of a conflict you currently have with time management where you don't enthusiastically agree on what to do at a certain time this week. Your goal is enthusiastic agreement and you must not do anything with that time until such an agreement is reached.

After you have defined the conflict (he wants to use the time to do this, but she wants to do that), begin your negotiation with prayer. Ask the Lord to give you his spirit of unity to find a resolution to the conflict that takes the interests and feelings of both of you into account. Also ask him to help you make your discussion safe and enjoyable for both of you.

Then, listen to each other's reasons for how each of you wants to spend the time. Be respectful and empathetic with each other, but don't diminish your own interests and feelings on the topic. Lay out for each other a roadmap that might lead to your own enthusiastic agreement.

After you understand each other's perspectives, brainstorm. How could the interests of both of you be accommodated by the same solution? In most cases, the issue will come up again in the future, so you might test a possible solution to find out how you both respond to it. If both of you are happy with the outcome when you try it, it's the solution you'll use in the future. If not, go back to brainstorming.

We suggest you take every conflict with time management seriously. Look over each other's schedules in advance to see if there is something planned that will be a problem for one of you. The more you practice negotiating, the faster you'll come to enthusiastic agreements about the way you spend your time.

— **Day 5** —

Perhaps you went through yesterday's exercise and decided your career is not a problem when it comes to scheduling your time. You were able to resolve conflicts over time management by making adjustments to your present career. Great! You have drawn appropriate boundaries around your work life, and you have allowed ample time to meet each other's emotional needs, have quality family time together, and achieve other important objectives.

But if your career doesn't give you enough time to make your marriage fulfilling, we strongly recommend a career change. When you consider the career paths of most people, they usually change several times during their lifetime. One way or another, your career is likely to change during *your* lifetime. Are you willing to change your career path to help achieve your most important objectives in life, or will you let some of the random factors of life make those changes for you?

When couples first hear this idea, many of them think we're nuts to suggest such a thing. But we're firm believers that your career should support your spouse and family—not the other way around. What if the career itself causes you or your spouse to lose your love for each other? Then your career is defeating its very purpose. Instead of creating a fulfilling lifestyle, it's creating a miserable lifestyle.

We're not blind to the realities of life; a change in career might mean a big step backward financially. It may require extensive retraining. You may need to limit extras, or even downsize to a smaller home. But isn't a loving marriage more valuable than any of those things? If your career is hurting your marriage, it's time to make some changes to your career.

We encourage you to discuss your schedules together each week, making sure you agree on how to use your time. That's an essential part of two becoming one. And don't neglect each other. Make sure that your schedule includes spending fifteen hours together so you can build a deep and lasting marriage. God's given you a "good work" to do in caring for each other. Don't let activities or responsibilities of lesser importance crowd out the time it takes to stay in love.

PRAYER FOR THE WEEK

Father, if our current career paths are undermining the good work you have for us to do, please help us find an alternative path that would support it. Help us to be honest with each other when our schedules create a problem for either of us. Give us a spirit of humility, patience, compassion, and sympathy as we try to resolve conflicts in the way we want to schedule our time. Above all, we want to honor you in the decisions we make, so please help us to be mindful of the plans you have for us, and to keep our hope and trust in you.

Week 23

Money Matters

No one can serve two masters. Either he will hate the one and love the other, or he will be devoted to the one and despise the other. You cannot serve both God and Money.

Matthew 6:24

Betsy's husband, Mel, kept all of their investments in his name: savings accounts, money market accounts, and stocks. As a result, she had no idea that he had managed to save over forty thousand dollars until she saw a stray bank statement on his desk one afternoon. Given her new discovery, Betsy couldn't understand why Mel was telling her they couldn't afford to have children yet and should keep saving. When she confronted Mel, he blew up. "You wouldn't understand even if I tried to explain it to you!" he exploded. The next day, Betsy opened her own checking account and refused to hand over any more money to Mel.

When they were dating, Brad loved buying little gifts for Marianne; she would light up with each new trinket. In their early years of marriage, he justified her purchases as necessary for their new home. Brad made a good living; but before long, Marianne's addiction to shopping was leading her to spend far more than they could afford. Marianne had not been able to stick to a budget, and Brad responded by taking away her credit cards and taking her name off the checking account. This infuriated Marianne, who felt he was treating her like a child.

Eric and Amanda were both committed to using their resources for God's glory, and sought his wisdom in how they spent their money. They followed a budget that included donations to their church and other ministries. After a friend joined a particular ministry devoted to the homeless, Eric wanted to direct all of their giving toward that ministry. Amanda was hesitant since they had other friends who counted on their financial support in their work as missionaries. Eric felt very passionate about it, and said to Amanda, "Come on! This ministry is just getting started, and it really needs our help to succeed. Don't you care about the homeless downtown at all?"

Day 1

All couples have conflicts over finances from time to time; indeed, some people claim it's the number one cause of divorce. But the truth of the matter is that financial conflicts don't cause divorce— it's the *way* couples try to resolve their conflicts, including financial ones, that can end a marriage. When couples argue about money but never find solutions, or when they make independent decisions about its use, they can create huge resentment and damage each other's feeling of love. On the other hand, if financial conflicts are discussed respectfully and honestly, with mutual agreement as the goal, a couple's love for each other can grow, no matter how dire the financial forecast might be.

Your care for each other should be among your highest priorities. But if money is more important to you, especially if it's your highest priority, then you will be tempted to fall into the trap of either arguing about financial conflicts or making independent decisions. The only way for you to resolve financial conflicts in a healthy way is to care more for each other than you care about money.

Do you and your spouse have disagreements over financial planning? Have you ever experienced conflicts similar to any of the scenarios that started this week's readings? To have a thriving marriage, you need to be more concerned about Love Bank withdrawals than the withdrawals from your checking account. So start this week with a time of prayer, asking God to make your marriage your top priority, regardless of your financial concerns.

—— Day 2 ——

Money is mentioned in the Bible more than eight hundred times. In one of the most definitive verses about God's position on money, Jesus is quoted as saying:

> No one can serve two masters. Either he will hate the one and love the other, or he will be devoted to the one and despise the other. You cannot serve both God and Money. (Matt. 6:24)

Christ's point is that you can't make money your top priority and also make serving God your top priority. In fact, the impression we get reading other sayings of Christ (Matt. 6:19–21) is that accumulating money should not be anywhere close to the top of our list of priorities.

God designed principles for using money and thinking about possessions for our benefit. He knows how susceptible we are to idolizing the material things we have in our lives, so he has provided guidance and wisdom to help us put money in its proper place—in service to God, and for our well-being and comfort.

As we consider marital conflicts that often arise about finances, keep God's position on this topic in mind. If you understand that

God has given you material possessions and money to provide for your comfort and to serve his kingdom, then you will share the mind of Christ as you approach these conflicts together.

Day 3

When a couple first comes to see me for counseling, I often ask them how they make their financial decisions. Consider your own answers to these questions:

Do you have a joint checking account?

Does the money that both of you earn go into that account?

Do you make decisions together on how that money is to be spent?

Do you take each other's feelings into consideration when making purchases?

For most of the couples I counsel, that isn't the way it's done at all. In most of the rocky marriages I see, each spouse makes independent decisions about how money is to be spent. Then they fight about the effects of those decisions on each other.

If a couple cares for each other, and wants to avoid Love Bank withdrawals, they should be guided by the Policy of Joint Agreement whenever they make financial decisions. The money both spouses earn should be deposited into a joint checking account, but no check should be written or purchases made unless they are both in enthusiastic agreement. When there's a conflict, as there is sure to be, the couple should respectfully negotiate a solution, keeping each other's interests in mind.

When you face financial conflicts in your own marriage, we encourage you to begin those discussions with prayer. Ask for God's wisdom to find a resolution that not only satisfies each other, but also fits the plan he has for your lives. Remember: the Lord has provided your money. Are you in the habit of asking him how he'd like you to spend it?

—— Day 4 ——

Yesterday, we challenged you to put God's will at the heart of your discussions. But what does this look like on a practical level?

God wants you to value your relationship more than your money. So whenever you have a conflict over finances, sit down with each other and find a resolution that will make both of you happy. First of all, keep your conversation pleasant and safe. After you have prayed together, discuss the issue with honesty and respect, trying to understand each other's opinions and feelings. Then you should search for a solution that would work for both of you. If you can't agree right away, the money stays in the account until an enthusiastic agreement is reached. Don't settle for a reluctant agreement—that will usually lead to resentment because it will erode your love for each other. As you brainstorm, give each other's ideas a chance to work on a tentative basis. If it works, you've found the solution. If not, go back to brainstorming.

This is a very difficult assignment for many couples at first. But after they practice for a while, and come to understand each other better, they become skilled at resolving financial conflicts on the run. We can usually resolve these conflicts within minutes when we're considering financial decisions together as a couple.

Your care for each other is far more important than any financial decision. Your marriage will not be ruined by delaying a purchase—it's making purchases without agreement that will cripple you. When you buy something that makes your spouse feel uncomfortable, you have valued that item above your spouse's comfort and security. But if you negotiate until you are both enthusiastic about the purchase, then you will have proven your care rather than your thoughtlessness.

We think it's helpful to first practice these negotiating skills on insignificant or hypothetical situations, when your emotions are not running high and little is at stake. So take some time to hone those conflict resolution skills today: discuss one of the scenarios that opened this week's readings. What was unhealthy about that couple's approach to financial conflict? How would you handle the situation differently?

Day 5

When emotions run high, even the most sincere and generous person can turn to making disrespectful judgments against their spouse to try to get their way. It might be formed as an accusation ("You could care less about helping the homeless shelter.") or phrased as a demeaning question ("Do you have to buy every pair of shoes you see?"); the result is always the same. Your spouse will be offended. When it comes to financial stress, such comments easily slip off the tongue. If you've made such statements in the past, it's time to acknowledge those mistakes, apologize, and commit to avoiding such statements in the future.

God has prepared good work for your money, and that can include a variety of uses, from saving for unexpected expenses and paying off debts to helping a needy neighbor or supporting a new ministry. Sometimes a spouse may feel convinced their cause must be God's best plan for their money. But don't make the mistake of thinking God's will is more important than the success of your marriage. God's will *is* the success of your marriage. So you need to negotiate decisions together, with prayer, until you both feel confident about God's desire for your money.

As you end the week, reflect on James 1:17: "Every good and perfect gift is from above, coming down from the Father of the heavenly lights, who does not change like shifting shadows." How can this verse's perspective help you make wise decisions about handling money in your marriage?

⟶ PRAYER FOR THE WEEK ⟵

Father, we know everything we have comes from you. It's easy to get caught up in our needs and wants, and to make money more important than it should be. Help us to make financial decisions that honor you. Show us how to budget our money for your glory, and how to work together to decide how to use it. And help us to be understanding toward each other, exhibiting a sincere desire to see things from the other's perspective. Please make these guidelines for negotiation second nature for us, that we might resolve conflicts in a way that honors you and builds our love for each other.

Week 24

When Your Kids Come between You

Unless the LORD builds the house,
　　its builders labor in vain.
Unless the LORD watches over the city,
　　the watchmen stand guard in vain.
In vain you rise early
　　and stay up late,
toiling for food to eat—
　　for he grants sleep to those he loves.
Sons are a heritage from the LORD,
　　children a reward from him.

　　　　　　　　　Psalms 127:1–3

When Jordan was growing up, her parents believed in firm discipline. If she was defiant or disobedient, she knew that she would receive a spanking, followed by a talk and time of prayer with her mom or dad and, finally, a hug. Her parents felt they would be doing Jordan a disservice if they didn't provide clear correction, and they took their disciplinary role very seriously.

Jordan thought her parents had raised her well, and planned to take the same disciplinary approach with her children.

Then she married Ben, who felt children should not be spanked at all. He had been raised by a father who was physically abusive to him, and so he vowed never to put his children through what he'd experienced.

Jordan understood Ben's past, and reluctantly agreed to raise their children with no spankings. But when she found herself the stay-at-home mom of two toddlers who were becoming increasingly unmanageable, she blamed their incorrigibility on Ben's refusal to allow spanking.

Instead of negotiating with each other to find mutually acceptable alternatives to spanking, they argued with each other. In one of their fights, Ben accused Jordan of wanting to do to their children what his father had done to him. "I do not!" she responded angrily. "But I also don't want to raise two spoiled kids! I'm starting to think you don't really love them or me—you're just taking the easy way out by avoiding the problem!" Their arguments not only made it more difficult for them to find a good alternative to spankings—they also made massive Love Bank withdrawals. Their differing opinions about childrearing were quickly ruining their marriage.

Day 1

Spouses often butt heads over the best way to raise their children. When spouses have had very different experiences growing up, or when one has suffered abuse, it can make it seem impossible to come to an agreement regarding child discipline. Even when a couple agrees on disciplinary methods prior to having children, the reality of life with little ones can throw all of their best theories out the window.

Consider Ben and Jordan's situation. Jordan was trying to be considerate of Ben's feelings. Since they could not agree on spankings, she refrained from using them to discipline their children.

But this led to resentment on her part because she felt that the lack of spankings was allowing her children's behavior to get out of control. If Jordan had acted independently by ignoring Ben's concerns and spanking the children, *he* would have experienced resentment about her decision to ignore his wishes, probably for the rest of his life.

So were they in a no-win situation? We don't think so.

Jordan and Ben spent all their energy on emotional arguments that were full of disrespect and anger but empty of real solutions. What they really needed was some respectful negotiation. Brainstorming together, they could have developed a mutually acceptable approach to discipline that eliminated resentment on both ends.

Have you faced any conflicts about children in your marriage? Take some time to pray about your children today, asking God to help you raise them well—in a way that makes you both feel comfortable.

Day 2

We read in Psalm 127:3, "Sons are a heritage from the LORD, children a reward from him." We all know that children are a blessing, and most of us are grateful when they arrive. But they can also create a lot of stress for their parents. The psalmist seems to understand this dynamic when he writes:

> Unless the LORD builds the house, its builders labor in vain. Unless the LORD watches over the city, the watchmen stand guard in vain. In vain you rise early and stay up late, toiling for food to eat—for he grants sleep to those he loves. (vv. 1–2).

Unless the Lord builds the house—the house of your family and your children—it's all in vain. And unless it's God guarding your little "city," it's all in vain. And then there's that last part, "toiling for food to eat." Are you ever worried about whether you're doing the right things for your family? We've all been there in some way.

The bottom line is that the Lord is faithful, and he is the one who "grants sleep to those he loves." Are you resting in the knowledge that your children belong to God? Do you feel confident in his faithfulness to help you raise your family? Or do you take the entire burden of your children turning out right on your own shoulders?

God has given these children to you as a gift. When you are overwhelmed by the responsibilities of parenting, or you face conflicts concerning your children, turn to the One who gave them to you. He is faithful. He is watching over you. And no matter what happens, you and your family are in his loving hands. If you belong to him, nothing can separate you from his love (Rom. 8:38–39).

Day 3

The fact that children make marriage more difficult is well documented. Statistics show that the more children a couple raises, the more likely they are to divorce. There are many reasons for this effect, but the most important reason is that caring for children leaves spouses with less time and energy to meet each other's emotional needs. And when those needs go unmet, spouses lose their love for each other. Parents can be so committed to the care of their children that they forget to care for each other.

Children can also be hard on marriages because conflicts over children are usually among the most difficult to resolve. We love our children, and it's especially tempting to act independently of our spouse when we are concerned about their well-being. When parents don't agree on how to punish a child for disobedience, however, a unilateral decision by either one is almost certain to be offensive. When one becomes the disciplinarian and the other becomes the protector of the children, the spouse doing the protecting often feels the pain of the discipline more acutely than the children do. The one doing the disciplining feels abandoned and unappreciated. And it's not just discipline that can cause resentment—unilateral giving of favors or rewards without agreement can cause resentment as well.

How have children affected your marriage? Discuss with each other how your marriage has changed—for better or worse—since your kids arrived. Have you kept your care for each other a top priority, even amidst the pressures of parenting?

Day 4

Conflicts over child training may seem impossible to resolve. But it's important—for both the sake of your children and the health of your marriage—to resolve those differences and develop a unified approach to parenting. When a conflict arises, don't do anything until you have come to an agreement. Begin your negotiation with prayer and assure each other that you will be pleasant and you will make the discussion safe, avoiding selfish demands, disrespectful judgments, and angry outbursts. Listen carefully to understand each other's perspective. Then brainstorm and test some solutions that may lead to your mutual enthusiasm—whether it's a new form of punishment, appropriate rewards for your child, or combinations of both. If a test fails to provide an enthusiastic agreement, go back to brainstorming.

As you negotiate, reflect on the verses from Psalm 127 that we discussed earlier: ultimately, your children belong to the Lord, and he has a plan for them. He will be faithful to them. Your job is to raise them in a way that is mutually agreeable to both of you, because your parenting should strengthen your marriage—not undermine it. Trust God with your children, and raise them to love and honor him. If you both share this mind-set, your conflicts over childrearing will be much easier to resolve.

Have you been an effective parenting team, working together to discover God's will for your children? Or has one of you taken a unilateral approach to childrearing? Talk about your parenting roles with each other today and ask God to help you make wise parenting decisions that you can put into practice together.

Day 5

As we did last week, we recommend that you practice your negotiating skills with this issue. It's easier to have effective parenting discussions when you've practiced negotiating hypothetical situations before facing those real-life situations that get your adrenaline pumping. Try role-playing Ben and Jordan's dilemma that we read about earlier this week, or create another hypothetical conflict about childrearing to discuss. Make your discussion enjoyable, avoiding any selfish demands, disrespectful judgments, or angry outbursts. Think about how trusting God with their children might help this couple find agreement.

After you finish your role playing, think about how you and your spouse have tried to resolve real-life conflicts over childrearing in the past. Have you ever resorted to making selfish demands or disrespectful judgments about each other's parenting? Have you ever let your anger get the best of you? If so, you should apologize and commit yourselves to eliminating these love-destroying tendencies.

Now look at the present. Have you been honest with each other with how you feel about each other's childrearing practices? If you feel resentful about any of each other's parenting habits, share your feelings now. Work as a team to brainstorm some new parenting strategies you can both feel enthusiastic about. We want you to tackle the challenges of parenting without losing your love for each other. And that ultimately gives your children one of the best parenting gifts of all: a mom and dad who are in love.

ꙮ PRAYER FOR THE WEEK ꙮ

Father, we trust you with our children and with our family. We know that you are watching over us and that you have a plan for us and for our children. Help us work together, with the guidance of your Spirit, to find the best ways to raise our children. Help us to avoid being angry with them, to be consistent in our training methods, and to teach them to love and honor you.

Week 25

Can't We Just Cuddle?

Developing an Affectionate Relationship

Husbands ought to love their wives as their own bodies. He who loves his wife loves himself. After all, no one ever hated his own body, but he feeds and cares for it, just as Christ does the church—for we are members of his body.

Ephesians 5:28–30

When I travel without Joyce, I often find little notes she has packed among my clothes. In those notes, she tells me she loves me, of course. But the notes also send another message: Joyce would like to get the same little notes from me. So I have tried to leave behind similar notes for her when I'm able—sometimes on her pillow, for example.

My need for affection is not the same as Joyce's, nor is it met in similar ways. So I've had to discover these differences and act accordingly. For example, when we walk through a shopping center, it is important to Joyce that we hold hands, something that would never occur naturally to me. But Joyce has encouraged me to take her hand, and I'm glad to do so, because I know she enjoys it and it communicates to her something she wants to hear from me—that I love and care about her.

When I try to explain this kind of handholding to some husbands in my counseling office, they may question my manhood a bit. Isn't my wife "leading me by the nose," so to speak? In my opinion, nothing could be further from the truth. If holding Joyce's hand in a shopping center makes her feel loved and cherished, I would be a fool to refuse to do it. I appreciate her coaching on the kind of affection she appreciates from me. I promised to care for Joyce when I married her, and I meant every word of it. So if she explains how I can best give her the care she wants, I'm willing to learn. I want her happiness—because that's what will keep our marriage healthy and strong.

Day 1

Do you remember the first time you held each other's hands? What about your first kiss? For most couples, these signs of affection go a long way toward cementing your dating relationship. They change the nature of the relationship, and love units start pouring into your Love Banks. But they don't accumulate equally. Affection usually makes much larger deposits in a woman's Love Bank than it does in a man's Love Bank.

This imbalance between men and women doesn't just apply to affection. It applies to all of the ten most important emotional needs that we introduced in week 2. Wives generally experience greater fulfillment from receiving affection, intimate conversation, honesty and openness, financial support, and family commitment. Husbands, on the other hand, usually have a greater need for sexual fulfillment, recreational companionship, physical attractiveness, domestic support, and admiration than their wives do.

It's no wonder that husbands and wives have so much difficulty meeting each other's needs. They are willing to do for each other what they appreciate the most—but it turns out that what they appreciate most, their spouses appreciate least!

It's our position that husbands and wives should meet each other's important emotional needs regardless of how unimportant they are to the one meeting the need. By meeting those needs, each spouse makes massive deposits into each other's Love Banks, maintaining their feeling of romantic love for each other. If they fail to meet those needs, they will not only lose their romantic love, but they will also find their marriage to be very frustrating and unfulfilling.

We'll be looking closely at each of the ten needs throughout the weeks ahead, so start this week with a prayer, asking God to help you discover your spouse's unique combination of emotional needs—and how you can best meet them.

--------- **Day 2** ---------

Jokes abound on how, almost immediately after the wedding, a wife has to find her own way in and out of cars, restaurants, and so on. But a sensitive husband will open the door for her at every opportunity. It's a way to tell her, "I love you and care about you. I don't want anything to happen to you." That's what affection symbolizes to most women: it gives them a sense of security, protection, comfort, and approval from their spouse.

Many women express a need for physical closeness, such as hugging, handholding, and sitting close together in the evening. Kissing is very important to most women, as are token gifts and cards that express emotional attachment and commitment, or a thoughtful invitation to go out to dinner. Back rubs and foot massages are also favorites of many women who crave affection. Walks after dinner, a bouquet of flowers, phone calls, and conversations with thoughtful and loving expressions all add units to the Love Bank.

As more than one song has said, "There are a thousand ways to say I love you."

Most women see these affectionate actions as the essential cement of a relationship with a man. Without it, a wife usually feels alienated from her mate. With it she becomes bonded to him—and all the while, it strengthens her feeling of love for him.

How have you expressed affection in your own relationship? What do those affectionate acts mean to your spouse? Sometimes an act of affection can be annoying rather than comforting, so learn how to express your affection in a way that clearly communicates your care.

Find several ways you can show each other affection this week. At the end of the week, ask each other what made you feel loved and cared for the most.

—————————————— **Day 3** ——————————————

Affection is largely symbolic, a reminder of our caring love. But if our love is not put into action, the symbols of affection mean nothing. In week 2 we introduced Scripture that offers a wonderful picture of caring love, and it's appropriate to mention it again in the context of affection: "Love is patient, love is kind. It does not envy, it does not boast, it is not proud. It is not rude, it is not self-seeking, it is not easily angered, it keeps no record of wrongs" (1 Cor. 13:4–5).

The meaning of this passage can be amplified by taking every adjective—patient, kind, etc.—and turning them into verbs. So, it would look something like this: Love is *being patient,* love is *being kind.* Love is *not being envious, not boasting, not being proud.* Love is *not being rude* and *not looking out only for yourself.* Love is *not being easily angered* and *not keeping track of how the other person has wronged you.* It helps us see what caring love looks like in action.

Are you being patient with each other? Are you being kind? If so, your hugs will convey the care you are showing each other. But if you are being rude, easily angered, and keeping track of how your spouse has wronged you, a kiss means very little.

Look over the list of loving actions in 1 Corinthians 13 today. Are there any that require attention? Ask God to help you make your affection meaningful by putting your love into practice.

--------- Day 4 ---------

We've been looking this week at what affection is—a symbolic expression of care. But sometimes couples—particularly husbands—are confused about what it isn't. For a lot of men, affection is viewed as sexual foreplay, and they mistakenly assume it has the same arousing effect on women. So when men are affectionate, they often try to turn it into a sexual experience.

But that kind of affection does not communicate, "I care about you." Instead, it communicates, "I want sex." Instead of giving, it's taking. That selfish message is not lost to most women who crave affection. They deeply resent the use of such an important symbol of care if it's given *only* when their husbands have a need for sex.

So what is the basic difference between affection and sex? Think of it this way: affection is the environment of a marriage, while sex is an *event*. Affection is a way of life, a canopy that covers and protects a marriage. It's a direct and convincing expression of care that gives the event of sex a more appropriate context. Most wives need to know they are being cared for with acts of affection before sex means much to them. So whenever you and your spouse come together, a big hug and kiss should be routine whether or not there would be any possibility for sex later. In all of your interactions together, the way you touch each other, talk to each other, and treat each other should say, "I really care about you and I know you care about me."

Husband, ask your wife today whether she receives affection from you apart from sex. Do you have any "affectionate" habits that annoy

166

her because they communicate sexual desire instead of making her feel loved? Wife, be honest. (Occasionally, the roles will be reversed, but that's fairly unusual.) Then spend some time focused on expressing affection apart from the bedroom.

Day 5

Let's take a look at Ephesians 5:28–30 today:

> Husbands ought to love their wives as their own bodies. He who loves his wife loves himself. After all, no one ever hated his own body, but he feeds and cares for it, just as Christ does the church—for we are members of his body.

What does it mean to "love your wife as your own body"? It means that you take care of her needs the way you would take care of your own. The next phrase builds on that theme: "He who loves his wife loves himself." Whatever you do for your wife, you are also doing for yourself—you have become one entity, remember?

But this concept that what you do for your wife you are doing for yourself has profound meaning when it comes to this week's topic, affection, and next week's topic, sexual fulfillment. That's because affection is the necessary environment for sexual fulfillment. When a husband meets his wife's need for affection, he is also helping her meet his need for sexual fulfillment.

Husbands don't usually let a lack of conversation or affection get in their way of enjoying sex. They don't need conversation or affection to enjoy a sexual experience with their wife. On the other hand, if a wife doesn't feel very close to her husband because he hasn't been very talkative or affectionate lately, she will usually resist having sex with him. If your marriage is struggling sexually, affection may be one of the missing elements.

God has created us all with emotional needs—and he's designed marriage as a way we can meet those needs for each other. When a husband shows his wife affection, he honors God's plan for marriage. And next week we'll see how wives can reciprocate by meeting their husband's sexual needs. As you end this week, evaluate your relationship: Have you been feeling loved and cared for by your spouse? Ask God to give you both a deeper desire to fulfill each other's intimate emotional needs.

PRAYER FOR THE WEEK

For the husband:

Lord, if I have failed my wife by not showing her enough affection, open my eyes to ways I can serve her and love her by being affectionate in ways that mean the most to her. And help me avoid trying to be affectionate in ways that annoy her. Help me to be faithful to her and to you by showing her this affection. Strengthen our marriage by binding us together with love and affection toward each other.

For the wife:

Lord, sometimes I expect my husband to meet needs that I never tell him about. Show me how to be honest about my needs, and to express them in a nondemanding and respectful way. When he makes an effort to show me affection, help me to respond to him with the same care. Thank you for the gift of our marriage.

Week 26

The Fountain of Love

How to Meet the Need for Sexual Fulfillment

> May your fountain be blessed,
>   and may you rejoice in the wife of your youth.
> A loving doe, a graceful deer—
>   may her breasts satisfy you always,
>   may you ever be captivated by her love.
>   Proverbs 5:18–19

If you ever doubted it, this passage makes it clear: God wants you to enjoy sex! He has designed marriage to be intimate and passionate, and for you and your spouse to fulfill each other's deepest needs. Last week, we focused our attention on one of a wife's most important needs: the need for affection. This week, we will shift our attention to the most important emotional need for most men: sexual fulfillment.

Some women have a sex drive that is every bit as strong as their husband's. But in most cases, the husband's sex drive is much greater. This advantage can be explained physiologically. Men produce the aphrodisiac hormone testosterone in abundance, while women produce much less. This gives most men a much more intense craving for sex.

For women, however, the primary reason for sex is to create emotional bonding.

Is it any wonder that a husband and wife can have great difficulty trying to adjust to each other sexually? One has an ongoing craving for the sex act itself, while the other views it as a special event that demonstrates their love for each other. One wants sex to be brief, frequent, and spontaneous, while the other would like it to take more time, be less frequent, and follow a sequence of events that makes her feel emotionally connected. Is it possible to keep them both satisfied? God seems to think so. And so do we. So as you work through this week's devotions, we pray that you'll start to look like the lovers of Proverbs 5, feeling "ever captivated" by each other's love.

Day 1

In Scripture, sex is generally described poetically. In Genesis 2:24 we read, "For this reason a man will leave his father and mother and be united to his wife, and they will become one flesh." This describes both marriage and sex—it is a union of two bodies, two hearts. It's a beautiful image.

Then we move to Proverbs, where the author uses every imaginable water reference to describe sex:

> Drink water from your own cistern, running water from your own well. Should your springs overflow in the streets, your streams of water in the public squares? Let them be yours alone, never to be shared with strangers. May your fountain be blessed, and may you rejoice in the wife of your youth. (5:15–18)

In this passage, we are being warned not to drink from the public wells, but instead to enjoy our very own private well, the pure fountain of love we have with each other in marriage. Isn't that beautiful? Can't you sense the refreshment the Lord has provided for you through sex? Drink deeply.

The language of poetry is helpful for us to think about the mystery of sex—the profound unity of two people. But when it comes to the "how" of sex, and when a couple wants more from their sexual experience, then a less-poetic description might be helpful. So this week, we encourage you to talk openly about what you enjoy in your lovemaking and what you might like to change.

Have you been feeling satisfied with your sexual experiences lately? For some couples, this feels like an awkward question. But the more you talk about it with respect and a willingness to understand and accommodate each other, the better your sexual experiences will be.

—— Day 2 ——

We'd like to ask you a fundamental question today: Why do you have sex? We've already mentioned that the primary reason most men have sex is to relieve their sexual craving, while women have sex to create emotional bonding. Your own reasons may not be as simple as these. But your answers to this question will have a tremendous bearing on how and how often you will want to have sex.

Once you and your spouse have discussed why you want to have sex, consider this question: How should we have sex? We're talking about times and places and positions here—all of the details of what your sexual experience together might look like.

If left to their own devices, most men would choose a method of sex that reflects their purpose, which is to satisfy an intense craving. They would initiate a sex act by doing whatever it takes to create sexual arousal for themselves. This might include looking at and feeling their wife's body. The timing of sex might be before going to sleep, upon awakening, or any time in between. The sex act itself usually involves intercourse, but many men prefer oral sex because they find it to be quicker and more intense.

Based on a wife's perspective that sex should be a bonding experience, she would want sex to be part of a much larger romantic experience. Dining, dancing, romantic movies, and moonlit walks, all generously infused with affection and conversation, are examples of the foreplay that would lead her to a fulfilling sexual experience.

Not all husbands and wives behave the same way, and your motives may not even be close to what I've described. So take some time today to explain to your spouse how you feel about sex. What way of making love with your spouse would please you the most if he or she agreed to it enthusiastically?

Day 3

Given their different motivations and preferences, it can be difficult for a husband and wife to reach an enthusiastic agreement regarding how they have sex. Having sex his way makes her feel like a receptacle—something he uses merely to relieve his sexual craving. Having sex her way makes him feel she is imposing conditions that make sex far too complicated.

Scripture provides some guidance regarding this common marital conflict. In 1 Corinthians 7:3–5 Paul writes:

> The husband should fulfill his marital duty to his wife, and likewise the wife to her husband. The wife's body does not belong to her alone but also to her husband. In the same way, the husband's body does not belong to him alone but also to his wife. Do not deprive each other except by mutual consent and for a time, so that you may devote yourselves to prayer. Then come together again so that Satan will not tempt you because of your lack of self-control.

Paul is encouraging married couples to have sex when either spouse needs it. Why? Because sexual temptation is real and powerful if you don't meet each other's need for it. Don't deprive your partner of sex, leaving him or her open to temptation. Instead, fulfill each other's needs so that you will be protected and grow in intimacy.

Does this Scripture mean that whenever a husband has a desire for sex, his wife must immediately oblige, regardless of how she feels about it? What if she's asleep, or sick, or has an appointment to keep? This Scripture encourages none of that. It simply makes the point that a husband and wife should fulfill each other's need for sex. You aren't depriving each other of sex when you set conditions that make it enjoyable for both of you. In fact, the more you make sex mutually enjoyable, the more likely you will increase its frequency.

Have either of you been depriving the other of a fulfilling sexual experience? Have you been letting something get in the way of meeting each other's need for sex? If so, talk about why this happens. What could you do to make sex more convenient and desirable for you both?

——— Day 4 ———

Let's look at 2 Corinthians 9:7 today, where Paul reminds us that "Each man should give what he has decided in his heart to give, not reluctantly or under compulsion, for God loves a cheerful giver." In the same way, a husband should want his wife to make love to him "not reluctantly or under compulsion," but cheerfully. If he tries to force his spouse to have sex using guilt or coercion, that need will ultimately be met less often.

The best way to become "cheerful lovers" is to turn sex acts (a typical husband's preference) into sexual events (a typical wife's preference) as frequently as possible. When a husband meets his wife's needs for affection and intimate conversation, he creates the conditions that make sex an event for her. Those actions help her feel bonded to him emotionally, and sex adds an important dimension to her feeling of intimacy.

We encourage you to try something: give each other your undivided attention for three hours, meeting each other's needs for affection and intimate conversation, before making love for an hour. Couples who follow this advice usually report back that their relationship has definitely improved after trying it for just one week.

When a husband meets his wife's needs for affection and intimate conversation, she usually finds it much easier to meet his need for sexual fulfillment. Of course, the converse is also true. The more she meets his need for sexual fulfillment, the easier it is for him to meet her emotional needs for affection and intimate conversation. Rather than depriving each other, you become the one providing what your spouse needs most. Nothing builds romantic love quicker than that.

Have either of you ever felt "reluctant or under compulsion" when it comes to sex? Today, give some thought and discussion to what would make you feel like a more "cheerful" lover.

Day 5

Have you been following the Policy of Undivided Attention lately? This rule helps you meet each other's most important emotional needs (affection, sexual fulfillment, intimate conversation, and recreational companionship) and builds your love for each other in the most effective way possible. But this rule also helps turn a sexual act into a sexual event. If you get into the habit of giving each other fifteen hours of undivided attention every week, you will be able to increase your frequency of lovemaking with enthusiastic agreement.

We suggested yesterday that you talk with each other and be affectionate for three hours prior to making love. But we haven't seen your answers to the questions we asked earlier this week: Why should we have sex? How should we have sex? Your answers to those two questions may make our suggestions very inappropriate. Maybe she really doesn't want to talk and be affectionate for three hours. Maybe playing cards together first or going on a hike together (recreational companionship) would make her far more willing to make love.

It's up to you to create the environment that makes lovemaking attractive for both of you. The suggestion we made is based on the experience we've had with most couples. But if you don't fit the typical pattern, be creative and find the conditions that guarantee a frequent and enjoyable sexual experience with each other.

But don't take the position that sex just isn't for you. That would be "depriving" each other of an experience God wants you to have. When done right, marital sex is extremely important as a way to make massive Love Bank deposits into both of your Love Banks. It is the physical demonstration of two becoming one.

PRAYER FOR THE WEEK

Lord, you have given us the privilege and responsibility of meeting each other's sexual needs. We understand its importance to our marriage and we want to make it a priority. Help us create the conditions that make both of us willing to make love, and the creativity to make each experience enjoyable for both of us. Give us the courage to talk honestly with each other about this topic so we can meet each other's needs and deepen our relationship. Thank you for giving us everything that's good in life, and help us look to you when we find life to be difficult. Your goodness is abundant.

Week 27

Love Talks

My dear brothers, take note of this: Everyone should be quick to listen, slow to speak and slow to become angry.

James 1:19

When Terri returned home after her first date with Sean, she told her roommate all about their evening and what a great time she'd had. They'd gone to dinner at a charming little restaurant. Then they had strolled downtown, looking in shop windows, laughing about some funny things that had happened that week and about their crazy waiter. Finally, they had stopped for coffee and talked about some of their favorite books and movies. It had been a perfect evening.

Over the next several months, Sean and Terri continued to date each other, and when they were not physically together, they communicated daily through email, texting, and phone conversations. Hardly a day went by that they didn't make multiple contacts with each other. They were married within a year, and had a fairytale wedding and a wonderful honeymoon. Terri thought she was the luckiest woman in the world.

Their first year of marriage went very well, but something ominous began happening during their second year: they both started to engage in separate activities. Part of the reason for this change was that their jobs required they both work evenings—but they weren't the same evenings. Sean generally hit the gym after work for pick-up basketball on Thursday nights because Terri worked that night. Terri had a Bible study Tuesday night and dinner with her friends on Wednesdays because Sean worked those nights. What made matters even worse was that they would be called to work on other evenings and even weekends without much notice, ruining whatever plans they might have had to be together.

Over time, and very innocently, their work schedules crowded out their time together—and their conversation. And during the day they were now too busy to email, text, or call each other. Terri thought wistfully about their dating days, and how easy it had been for them to talk to each other. One evening she brought it up before bed, and said to Sean, "I really miss talking with you. I wish we could talk more, the way we used to."

"Sure, Terri," Sean replied, looking up from his computer. "What would you like to talk about?"

That comment was not what Terri needed to hear. "I don't know." She faltered. "How was your day?" But inside, she thought, *If you need to ask, then what's the point? You never used to be at a loss for conversation!*

Sean told her a little about his day, and then turned his attention back to the computer. For Terri, it was worse than never talking at all; he didn't ask her about her day at all. She left the conversation believing Sean had lost his interest in her. *I guess that's what happens after being married*, she thought sadly.

Day 1

One question I often hear from wives is, "Why is it so difficult for my husband to have a simple conversation with me?" Part of the answer is that men do not tend to have as great a need for conversation as women. A woman usually longs to talk with her husband about the events of her day, people she may have encountered, and—most of all—*how she reacted to those experiences.* Men don't usually feel the same way.

But when a man is dating, he generally finds it easy to have this kind of conversation. He wants to get to know his girlfriend. He wants to understand her problems and figure out how he can help her overcome them. He tries to learn about her personal history, family, greatest achievements, and disappointments—and her past romantic relationships. In this same vein, he wants to discover how to be attractive to her. He promptly and regularly calls her whenever they cannot be together because this shows her how much he cares about her and thinks of her.

But, as many wives can testify, somewhere after saying "I do," a husband often loses his way. Does he feel he has learned everything there is to know about his wife? Has he decided that, now that he's married, he doesn't need to attract her with conversation or keep repeating how much he cares for her? Or, like Sean, does he simply become too busy and too tired to meet his wife's need for intimate conversation?

Many couples find their conversations dwindling after marriage, allowing precious love units to be drained from the wife's Love Bank. Is this happening in your relationship? Does your spouse have an important need for intimate conversation that's going unmet, making her feel unloved? Talk about these questions today and ask God to bless your devotional times with good conversation throughout the week ahead.

Day 2

What does Scripture say about our daily conversation as husband and wife? The whole book of the Song of Songs offers an example of passionate, rich conversation between married people. It's written as a masterful poem that describes what Solomon and his wife feel toward each other. You may not write poetry, but you can share all the things you love about each other in your own words. And you can do that every day.

But talking about what you love about each other isn't all there is to marital conversation. Since the content and quality of your conversation with each other is so important, let us offer you some guidance we like to call the four friends of intimate conversation.

The first friend of intimate conversation is to use it to *inform, investigate, and understand each other*. Communicating what you love about each other is part of this friend, but there are many more parts to consider. Inform each other about your history and everyday schedules. Investigate each other's personal feelings, interests, and activities. Try to understand what makes your spouse happy or sad. The more you learn about each other and use that information to support and adjust to each other, the more intimate your conversation becomes. One of the most valuable uses of marital conversation is to create emotional closeness, and nothing does that better than talking about each other in positive and encouraging ways.

The second friend is to *develop an interest in each other's favorite topics of conversation*. If you educate yourselves on topics that interest each other, it will not only broaden your horizons, but it will also help you understand each other better. When you are life partners, you should know what captivates the interest of your spouse.

These two friends of intimate conversation describe what you should be talking about: each other and your primary interests. Is this how you spend most of your time conversing with each other? If so, you probably feel very close and united. If not, you may feel alienated and certain you are growing apart. Discuss with each other how your conversation can become more intimate.

— Day 3 —

The third friend of intimate conversation deals with etiquette: *balance the conversation*. A conversation should be a two-way street—you talk and you listen.

We read in James 1:19, "My dear brothers, take note of this: Everyone should be quick to listen, slow to speak and slow to become angry." We'll focus on the "slow to become angry" part later this week, but for now consider the other two parts: be quick to listen, and slow to speak. Is this how you engage your spouse in conversation?

If your wife asks how your day was, do you use the opportunity to share about meaningful things going on in your life and then turn the question back and ask your wife about *her* day? Are you willing to drop the sports section or turn off the TV or close the laptop in order to really listen to your spouse? That's being quick to listen.

And are you slow to speak, or do you interrupt your spouse, eager to offer your own opinion? Do you finish your spouse's sentences in a way that never allows him or her to finish a thought? Or do you wait, really listening to your spouse's complete thought before formulating your response?

It's important to listen as your spouse shares the thoughts on his or her heart, and even ask good questions to draw out what he or she is thinking. Ask your spouse today if you are the kind of conversationalist described in James 1:19. Is there anything you could do to improve your listening skills?

Finally, the fourth friend of intimate conversation is to *give each other your undivided attention when you converse*. One of the quickest ways for a husband to infuriate his wife is to carry on a conversation with her while he's watching television. Your spouse can't experience meaningful conversation with you if you appear to be more interested in something else.

But that said, you still might need a little practice, especially if you're the husband. One of the best indicators of undivided attention is to look into each other's eyes as you talk to each other. For some, that can be a very difficult assignment. But the alternative of looking anywhere but at each other gives the impression you are not giving the conversation your fullest attention.

As we've encouraged you to do throughout this book, we recommend fifteen hours of undivided attention each week. I hold couples I counsel accountable to this, so I ask for an estimate from him, and an estimate from her. When they give me their estimates for the week, almost inevitably her estimate of time for undivided attention is less than his. I usually assume that her estimate is more accurate because women are usually more aware of what undivided attention is. So if your wife complains that you don't give her your undivided attention when you are talking together, take her word for it, and ask her to help you understand what she means by that.

Do you use the four friends of intimate conversation to keep your marriage healthy and fulfilling? Or do one or more of them need to be strengthened? Discuss the quality of your conversation with these four friends in mind.

Day 4

In Ephesians 4:29, we read, "Do not let any unwholesome talk come out of your mouths, but only what is helpful for building others up according to their needs, that it may benefit those who listen." So far, we have been encouraging you to make your conversations "benefit those who listen." But what about "unwholesome" conversations? We're not talking about dirty jokes or obscenities. We're talking about conversations that fail to build each other up and instead tear each other down. A steady diet of this kind of conversation doesn't do anyone any good. It discourages conversation.

We call "unwholesome" conversations the enemies of intimate conversation.

You've been introduced to the first three of these enemies already. They are making demands, being disrespectful, and expressing your anger during a conversation. And we hope you've already worked at eliminating them because they make huge Love Bank withdrawals. This week's Scripture (James 1:19) reminds us that anger should be avoided in our conversation.

But there's a fourth enemy of intimate conversation we have yet to discuss: *dwelling on your spouse's mistakes, past or present.*

By its very nature, intimate conversation provides an unobstructed view into each other's thoughts and feelings. And if one of you keeps thinking about the other's mistakes, you will want to talk about them. But as you have probably already noticed, if you talk about these offenses to each other, it ruins your conversation. An apology and commitment to avoid the mistake in the future should end the conversation.

Of course, if the mistake is repeated, there's nothing wrong with trying to keep it on the front burner. Talking about it is not dwelling on past mistakes if there has been no resolution. But when you do discuss the issue, remember to show respect and empathy for each other as you seek to negotiate a solution. And once the issue's been resolved, don't let it creep in and ruin future conversations.

Has your conversation been infected by any of the four enemies of intimate conversation: demands, disrespect, anger, or dwelling on past mistakes? If so, ask God to help you overcome those enemies so that your conversation can "benefit those who listen."

Day 5

The love chapter, 1 Corinthians 13, is packed with friends and enemies of intimate conversation. "Love is patient, love is kind." These qualities encourage intimate conversation. "It is not rude" (being disrespectful), "it is not easily angered" (expressing anger), "it keeps no record of wrongs" (dwelling on past and present mistakes). This is a description of how caring people talk to each other.

At the beginning of this chapter, and again at the end, Paul makes a startling point. He tells us that the care we show others is more important than anything else. In fact, it's even more important than understanding great mysteries of our faith or undertaking many good works. Without caring love, we are nothing.

In your marriage, your caring love is also the most important ingredient. And the way you care for each other is most vividly expressed in the way you talk intimately to each other. We sum up the friends and enemies of conversation in this way: *caring spouses converse in a caring way.*

We encourage you to incorporate intimate conversations into your married life. Take time to talk to each other about each other. Call and text each other spontaneously just to find out what the other person is doing. Identify each other's favorite topics of conversation and learn more about them to increase your interest. Balance your conversation so you are each talking and listening equally. Look at each other when you are talking together. Don't be distracted—give each other undivided attention.

When problems and conflicts arise, don't allow your conversation to turn negative with demands, disrespectful judgments, and angry outbursts. And don't keep bringing up mistakes that have already been addressed.

Take some time today to discuss any possible weaknesses in your conversation and what you might do to overcome them. Ask God to help you show your caring love for each other in the way you talk to each other.

PRAYER FOR THE WEEK

Father, we want our conversation to reflect our care for each other. Help us to learn more about each other, to develop a greater interest in each other's favorite topics, to balance our conversations, and to give each other undivided attention as we talk. We also ask you to help us overcome our pride and selfishness by eliminating demands, disrespect, and anger toward each other. And help us to keep no record of wrongs against each other, as you have forgiven us for our wrongs against you. Our faith and hope are in your Son, Jesus, and through him we have eternal life with you. But the greatest gift you have given us is love. Thank you for all three of these gifts.

Week 28

The Couple That Plays Together
Stays Together

And whatever you do, whether in word or deed, do it all in the name of the Lord Jesus, giving thanks to God the Father through him.

Colossians 3:17

While we were dating, we spent countless hours playing tennis. We both needed the exercise and it was my favorite way of getting it. Joyce agreed to play because she wanted to spend as much time with me as possible. But shortly after our marriage, Joyce announced, "Bill, I don't really enjoy tennis that much. I think I would prefer other ways of spending time together."

Joyce's confession came as a complete surprise to me. We had dated for six years before we married, and I thought she enjoyed tennis as much as I did. But after we were married, Joyce wanted us to be together without having to do things she didn't enjoy. So early in our marriage, she did the right thing. She let me know that tennis wasn't her favorite activity, and that she'd rather do something else together.

If you were in Joyce's position, would you have continued playing tennis with your husband, even though you didn't enjoy it that much? Or, if you were in my position, would you have continued to play tennis with someone else rather than give up the sport you enjoy most? Many couples would feel those are their only viable choices.

But we didn't make that decision. Instead, we chose a different path: we left tennis behind and found a new activity that we would both enjoy together. We switched from tennis to couples' volleyball, where we could play on the same team. It gave us plenty of exercise, and we both looked forward to playing together.

The outcome could have been quite different if we had chosen individual activities that were separate. We would have grown apart, each experiencing our most enjoyable moments of fun and relaxation without the other. But since we stuck together in pursuit of recreation, we're still each other's favorite recreational companions.

Day 1

Think back to your dating days. Were you each other's favorite recreational companions? You probably found yourselves attending events—sports, plays, symphonies, fishing trips, movies—you may not have attended on your own. But you were happy to do so, because you were getting to know this person who had your heart, and every opportunity to be together was worthwhile.

What happened after you were married? Did you keep up the same activities so you could be together? Or did you each drift to your own favorites without each other?

This week we're encouraging you to think about recreational companionship, an emotional need that tends to be especially important to men. It makes sense to include recreational companionship in the list of emotional needs. It's a craving for something that gives you emotional satisfaction when you have it, and makes you frustrated when you don't. You have a great opportunity to make massive deposits into each other's Love Banks simply by being with each other while enjoying leisure activities. Why squander that opportunity? And if you let someone else of the opposite sex make those deposits, you run a great risk of being unfaithful.

Marriage is two becoming one, and this premise should apply to every aspect of a couple's life together, including their recreational activities. It's also an important—and enjoyable—way to sustain your love. Are you still each other's favorite recreational companions? Whether your answer is yes or no, start this week with a prayer, asking God to help you discover some new ways to enjoy each other's company this week.

Day 2

Have you ever thought about the fact that your recreational time is part of your overall walk with God? There is nothing you do in your life that is separate from your life in Christ. Colossians 3:17 sums it up this way: "And whatever you do, whether in word or deed, do it all in the name of the Lord Jesus, giving thanks to God the Father through him." Whatever you do! That includes your work, your play, your worship, and your time with family and friends.

Now, what better way to use your downtime than to strengthen the unity of your relationship with your spouse? Remember Genesis 2:24? "A man will leave his father and mother and be united to his wife, and they will become one flesh." You and your spouse are one, and the way you choose to spend your recreational time should reflect that fundamental fact. After we married and I realized Joyce didn't enjoy tennis, I left my tennis game and we found a new sport we could both enjoy. It was part of being one. Instead of taking separate recreational paths, we chose a path that would allow us to have fun together. And we did it to the glory of God—because God is glorified whenever we strengthen our marriage.

Are you walking the same recreational path? Or have you been spending your recreational time apart and missing a chance to deepen your relationship? We encourage you to play together. It's a choice that will glorify God.

Day 3

Some couples can readily think of activities they enjoy doing together. If that's you, then plan for it! Put it on the calendar! And enjoy the time together.

Other couples are at a total loss when they try to think of activities to do together. If that's you, imagine that each of you stands in an invisible circle encompassing all your recreational interests. There are thousands of them: some you know about, and some you have yet to discover. If you work together with your spouse, you'll find that part of your circles overlap—and in that intersection are many recreational interests you could enjoy together.

We've made it easier for couples to discover these common recreational interests by offering the *Recreational Enjoyment Inventory*. You may make a free copy of it from the Questionnaires section of our marriagebuilders.com website. Just follow the directions. Once you find a few activities you both enjoy doing, start spending all of your recreational time doing them together, and you'll soon become each other's favorite recreational companions.

Day 4

Many wives are willing to sacrifice their own pleasure so their husbands can enjoy a particular activity. This may sound like a noble gesture. But what is the result? Deposits into his Love Bank create withdrawals in hers. A husband will often try to do the same thing.

But when he's doing something with his wife that only she enjoys, she is not becoming his favorite recreational companion.

So what should you do with activities that are done reluctantly or under compulsion for one of you? Let's look at 2 Corinthians 9:7 for a clue: "Each man should give . . . not reluctantly or under compulsion, for God loves a cheerful giver." In the same way, you want your spouse to be a *cheerful* recreational companion—someone who thoroughly enjoys joining you. So if you have not yet learned how to be each other's favorite recreational companions, here's a radical assignment: engage only in those recreational activities you and your spouse can enjoy together. This means you must rule out any activities you're doing together that your spouse doesn't truly enjoy, as well as any activities you're doing apart that only one of you enjoys.

You may think this idea sounds like a summons to misery and deprivation. But think it through. We are simply asking you to consider your spouse's feelings when selecting recreational activities from among those you already enjoy. It's possible to find recreational activities you can enjoy together just as much as each of you enjoys your current, separate recreational activities. You don't have to give up having fun—you will just start having fun together. In the process, you will be able to make Love Bank deposits almost effortlessly.

If you have already completed the *Recreational Enjoyment Inventory* we recommended yesterday, you will have identified a few activities that you might both enjoy. If you haven't had a chance yet to make a free copy of it, do that now so you can discover your common recreational interests. Then try our radical assignment: replace any activities you don't enjoy together with those you'll both enjoy.

Day 5

When we first introduced you to the Policy of Undivided Attention, we mentioned that fifteen hours per week should be spent meeting four emotional needs: affection, sexual fulfillment, intimate conversation, and recreational companionship. The first three would have made sense to you because they require undivided attention if they are to be met effectively. But what about recreational companionship? Why is that emotional need included with the others?

If you go back to your dating relationship, you'll remember that your courtship included recreational companionship. It provided the context for you to meet the other emotional needs that caused you to fall in love with each other. But it was a primary factor in itself for your falling in love, especially for the husband. So we include it in the fifteen hours you should spend together every week.

With undivided attention in mind, you'll find that some recreational activities cannot be considered part of your fifteen hours. That's not to say you shouldn't engage in these other activities together. It's just that when considering what to do during your time for undivided attention, make sure your recreational activity doesn't distract you from each other.

Dancing, card games, hiking, boating, and even working out at the gym together have been favorites of couples who want a recreational activity that provides an opportunity for undivided attention. But don't include friends with any of these activities. They'll distract you from each other. You should have as much privacy as possible during your fifteen hours.

Other recreational activities that include other friends or otherwise distract you from each other are a normal part of married life. We encourage you to engage in as many of these activities as possible. But these activities should be scheduled in addition to your fifteen hours of undivided attention. Don't ever let them replace the time you should be spending alone with each other.

PRAYER FOR THE WEEK

Thank you, Lord, for the joy we have in knowing each other, and in knowing you. Give us the wisdom to care for each other in ways that hit the target—ways that meet each other's most basic needs. Sometimes we get so wrapped up in our responsibilities in life that we forget to take time just to have fun together. So help us to not ignore our need for relaxation and recreation. Help us to use this "downtime" in ways that honor you, and in ways that strengthen our marriage. Help us take advantage of this challenge to become each other's favorite recreational companions.

Week 29

A Heart That's True

An honest answer is like a kiss on the lips.
Proverbs 24:26

When Zoe met Andrew, she found him to be one of the most charming men she had ever met. They had started chatting one day at a favorite local coffee shop, and after a few moments he had asked if he could pull up a chair. She was fascinated by his openness, and was equally delighted by his sincere interest in her. He asked for her phone number, and called the next day to ask her out to dinner.

Throughout their dating life, Zoe came to know Andrew as someone who would always tell her what was on his mind. And he never hesitated to answer any questions she had about him. He shared everything about himself with her, and did so with respect and candor. She found his honesty and openness very attractive, so attractive that it was one of the main reasons she fell in love with him. They married a year later, and Zoe was overjoyed that she would be living out her life with her best friend.

Their first year of marriage presented the usual challenges: finding a path that integrated their likes and dislikes, deciding how to divide the work around the house, figuring out how to spend time together. They succeeded, primarily because they spent quite a bit of their time talking honestly and openly with each other.

But as time went on, Zoe felt that Andrew shared less and less about himself. He was overwhelmed at work and didn't feel like talking about it at home. He also had some dreams about the future, but his lack of confidence in his ability to achieve his dreams kept him from sharing them with her. She would try to get him to open up more, but was disheartened by how little he volunteered. That honest quality she had found so attractive was slowly diminishing.

Day 1

Zoe fell in love with Andrew because she found his honesty and forthrightness so attractive. He shared openly, without screening anything or being defensive. He revealed his thoughts with humor and clarity, and Zoe loved it. But after marriage, she felt he was keeping part of himself from her, and she found that very unattractive. She didn't want to pry his thoughts out of him; she wanted him to share openly, allowing her to know him better than anyone else. Openness and honesty was one of her most important emotional needs.

Zoe is not unusual. The majority of women we have surveyed name honesty and openness as a significant emotional need. For them, radical honesty is not simply a tool for negotiation; it is a very attractive quality. A man who can allow his wife to see through to his soul without being disrespectful toward her, revealing himself to her with nothing held back, will remain attractive indeed.

What does Scripture say about the attractiveness of honesty? Proverbs 24:26 tells us, "An honest answer is like a kiss on the lips." When

Zoe received honest conversation from Andrew, it was like he was showering her with kisses. She experienced huge Love Bank deposits because he was meeting one of her most basic needs.

Husband, are you sharing your heart with your wife without making her work for it? Wife, when your husband volunteers information about his thoughts and feelings, does it draw you in and make him more attractive to you? Let you husband know what a difference this makes to you. If honesty is one of your wife's deepest needs, don't neglect giving her the "kiss on the lips" that comes from an honest answer.

Day 2

Some men will read this chapter and feel uncomfortable. *Why should I have to come home after a long day of work and share all of my thoughts? I just want to relax.* The simple answer to this question is this: you have been called to love your wife. In Ephesians 5:33 Paul instructs husbands, "each one of you also must love his wife as he loves himself." You want your needs to be met; if you love your wife as you love yourself, you will meet her needs. If she needs honest and open communication from you, free from defensiveness or disrespect, then it is essential for you to care for her in that way.

On the other hand, if this conversation is given grudgingly, you might as well skip it. Remember the principle from 2 Corinthians 9:7: "Each man should give what he has decided in his heart to give, not reluctantly or under compulsion, for God loves a cheerful giver." The same is true when it comes to giving to your spouse. It is essential that you meet this emotional need, and any other need for that matter, in a way that you enjoy; otherwise, it will not be effective and it will not become a habit.

Have either of you been reluctant about sharing your thoughts and feelings with each other? If so, how has that reluctance affected your relationship? What can you do to be open and honest without feeling reluctant? How can you be open and honest cheerfully?

Day 3

Hopefully, we've convinced you that it's important to meet your spouse's need for honesty and openness. But how can you do this cheerfully if it's not something you enjoy? Earlier, we mentioned two prime motivators for any act: enjoyment of the act itself, and enjoyment after performing the act. So if you want to meet your spouse's need for honesty and openness, you must either enjoy being honest and open or enjoy its consequences. Ideally, you should do both.

If you are tired when you first come home from work, this might not be a good time to meet that need. Instead, you might try setting aside time after dinner to talk about the day and what is going on in your heart. In addition to having a set time to reveal some of your inner thoughts, you might also offer them spontaneously when you they occur, by email, phone, or text message. At the end of the day, when you're lying in bed together, you might also feel like expressing some of your most private feelings. If it were followed by lovemaking, both prime motivators for being honest and open would come together to make it easier to do in the future.

Reflect on the idea of giving "cheerfully" to one another (2 Cor. 9:7). Are you meeting each other's needs out of a sense of obligation, or are you eager to meet each other's needs? What could you do to make sure the two primary forms of motivation are present when you meet the need for openness and honesty?

Day 4

Remember Andrew and Zoe? Their dating conversation was a beautiful example of intimacy. They shared thoughts and dreams, and offered each other encouragement. They rarely criticized each other, because they were focused on building each other up.

When Andrew started to avoid conversation after work, Zoe first responded with concern. Over time, however, her own hurt took over and she began making disrespectful judgments against Andrew. "Fine," she said, after one particularly quiet meal with an unresponsive Andrew. "Don't talk to me. You don't even care about this marriage."

Zoe felt justified in her actions, but she made conversation even more difficult for Andrew. Her accusation that he didn't care about their marriage made him feel defensive and misunderstood. "You have no idea of the stress I'm under!" he shouted in return. His angry outburst made everything worse. Zoe stomped to their room, slamming the door behind her. Andrew slept on the sofa that night.

A lack of openness and honesty between spouses can easily ignite Love Busters. When a spouse feels shut out, it's easy to respond with a selfish demand, a disrespectful judgment, or even an angry outburst. But these reactions only make the emotional openness they crave from their spouse even more elusive.

Have you ever reacted with Love Buster behaviors when you've felt a lack of openness or honesty from your spouse? How did your reaction affect your spouse? And what could you have done differently to encourage his or her openness?

—— Day 5 ——

Let's end the week with one final look at Zoe and Andrew's situation. Zoe knew that Andrew was stressed. But because he would not share the cause of his stress at work, she was left to wonder and imagine what was going on. She wondered what else he wasn't sharing with her. His lack of openness and honesty was driving a deep wedge between them. In keeping aspects of his life to himself, he was shutting Zoe out.

Husband, when you fail to let your wife into every aspect of your life, holding some areas as "private," you fail to meet her need for openness and honesty. But when you share freely, allowing your wife to know your joys, worries, stresses, plans, and hopes, you meet that need. And it's not to her benefit alone. When you share openly and honestly with your wife, you will find in her the confidant God enables her to be.

When God created Eve, it was in response to Adam's great need for companionship. God said, "It is not good for the man to be alone. I will make a helper suitable for him" (Gen. 2:18). Do you think you can live life to the fullest without the help of your wife? God did not design it to be that way. So as you become transparent with her, revealing your inner thoughts, daily activities, and plans for the future, watch as the Lord deepens your relationship and reveals the beauty of his plan for your marriage.

PRAYER FOR THE WEEK

Lord, we want to be open and honest with each other. Help us to find ways to enjoy meeting this essential need for each other. Please help us remove any obstacles that stand in the way of our open communication. Help us not to be self-protective or self-absorbed, but rather to share without defensiveness or judgment of each other. Knit us closer together as we reveal our inner thoughts, and build our marriage with intimacy and joy.

Week 30

The Laws of Attraction

Do you not know that your body is a temple of the Holy Spirit, who is in you, whom you have received from God? You are not your own; you were bought at a price. Therefore honor God with your body.

1 Corinthians 6:19–20

R ita was a vivacious woman who loved God with all of her heart. She had very good relationships with others, both men and women, but it had been a very long time since she had dated anyone—since high school. Rita was about eighty pounds overweight, and generally wore loose-fitting clothing to hide her figure. When she looked in the mirror, she reminded herself of the verses she knew about physical appearance. She had 1 Peter 3:3–4 taped to her mirror:

Your beauty should not come from outward adornment, such as braided hair and the wearing of gold jewelry and fine clothes. Instead, it should be that of your inner self, the unfading beauty of a gentle and quiet spirit, which is of great worth in God's sight.

Rita had a gentle, sweet spirit. But she wanted to be married.

On her twenty-eighth birthday, Rita decided she needed to lose weight to attract the kind of husband she wanted. She joined a gym, stocked the freezer with healthy frozen dinners, and set aside her favorite snacks in favor of fruits and vegetables. It took almost a year, but she got down to her goal weight and looked fantastic. Her phone started ringing, and soon she met Dave. After several months of dating, they were engaged, and they were married that winter.

Dave loved all of the snack foods Rita had given up. Happy and satisfied in her marriage, Rita let down her guard. She started missing workouts and took great joy in making his favorite meals. The pounds crept back on. Then, during her pregnancy with their first child, she found herself back at her old weight—and then beyond it.

After their son was born, Rita found herself too overwhelmed to stick to frozen dinners and her old workout routine. Around the house all day with a colicky baby, she began to turn to her favorite comfort foods. She began sinking into depression.

Dave was worried about Rita. Where was the beautiful woman he had married? When he suggested they go to the gym and diet together, she burst into tears. But he didn't let the issue go.

One night as he expressed his concerns, Rita retorted, "Look, Dave. You're a Christian man. I know you want to be like Christ. Well, the Bible says that 'The Lord does not look at the things man looks at. Man looks at the outward appearance, but the Lord looks at the heart.' So stop bothering me about what I look like! You should love me for who I am, not my appearance" (1 Sam. 16:7). After that, Dave gave up, but he felt Rita had deceived him, especially when he found out that she lost weight to find a husband.

Day 1

Some men do not care about physical appearance. Their wives can be overweight or underweight; it makes no difference. But Rita had not married one of these men. Dave had an emotional need for physical attractiveness and married her because she met that need. In fact, physical attractiveness was near the very top of his list of emotional needs.

Some women also express a need for physical attractiveness. We have known wives who have given their husbands the ultimate threat: either lose weight or go without sex. They find that he must look good if she is to be a "cheerful lover." Some wives are less concerned about appearance than health when they want their husband to lose weight. They live with the constant stress that their husband may die of something he could have prevented through diet and exercise.

Perhaps you are the one who has given up on your physical appearance. You want to be loved for who you are, not for how you look. We all feel that way to some extent. But for many people, especially men, having an attractive spouse meets a strong emotional need. And if their spouse makes no effort to look attractive, their Love Bank takes a hit.

Rita thought physical attractiveness was trivial because she didn't have that need. So she concluded that Dave's shallow sense of values was the culprit. If he would grow up and be more mature, he would look beyond her appearance. But this is not trivial to those who have it.

Discuss this very sensitive issue with each other. How important is physical appearance to each of you? Be honest in expressing your feelings and reactions. Then make a commitment to make the most of your physical health and appearance, in order to honor God and your marriage.

Day 2

Should physical appearance matter in a Christian marriage? There are many Christian men and women who let themselves go, convinced that their physical bodies are of little value. After all, God only looks at the heart, right?

It is true that Scripture places great value on character, much more than on physical appearance. But God tells us very specifically in 1 Corinthians 6:19–20 that our bodies matter:

Do you not know that your body is a temple of the Holy Spirit, who is in you, whom you have received from God? You are not your own; you were bought at a price. Therefore honor God with your body.

This passage sets out the foundational idea that our bodies don't belong only to us. God bought our bodies at a price. We should honor God by taking care of them, that we might be able to serve him to the best of our abilities. Have you ever thought about that before? Your health matters to God.

But your health also matters to your spouse. In 1 Corinthians 7:4 we read, "The wife's body does not belong to her alone but also to her husband. In the same way, the husband's body does not belong to him alone but also to his wife." Your body belongs to God and your spouse. And your physical appearance and health affect him or her.

It's easy in a Christian marriage to think that the spiritual is the only important part of life. Many Christian couples use the verses that Rita used to defend an unhealthy lifestyle. Afraid of being too caught up in the world's standards of beauty, they go to the other extreme and don't take care of themselves.

If you have not been taking good care of your body, then the ideas in this chapter may seem painful at first. But stick with it. Physical attractiveness is an important emotional need for most men and many women. We want you to have the best marriage possible, and to have the best life possible. So consider what we have to say. Ask God to give you an open spirit for the days ahead.

--- **Day 3** ---

We've found that the most crucial aspect of a person's physical attractiveness is their weight. To look attractive, your weight should be in the normal range—not too thin and not too fat. In fact, over 90 percent of the complaints we've heard in marriage about physical attractiveness has been about obesity. So we'd like to challenge both of you, for the sake of your health and your romantic love for each other, to get your weight down to a normal level.

If you need to lose weight, the formula for success is well known: you must burn more calories than you eat. And crash diets don't really do the job—you need a weight control program that becomes a way of life. All bodies are machines that burn fuel. So in order to lose weight, start with the right kind and amount of fuel. Eat nutritious foods and limit snacks. Resist the urge to take those extra portions.

Aerobic exercise will help you burn that fuel and lose those extra pounds while keeping your heart and lungs healthy. All it takes is enough exercise to elevate your heart rate for about thirty minutes every other day. But we've known many who exercise every day yet don't lose any weight. They're simply eating too much. If you have tried to lose weight in the past, but have failed, consider the lifestyle changes we're recommending.

We share the same diet program, and we also exercise with each other whenever possible. We encourage each other in weight control. And we recommend that you do the same. If you have agreed to lose weight, and keep it off, you must create a new lifestyle around diet and exercise, and you must both be a part of it. You may need to avoid foods that cannot be part of your husband's diet. Or maybe you need to join your wife in an exercise program.

Brainstorm with your spouse today about how you could create a healthy lifestyle together.

Day 4

While weight control is the major factor in maintaining physical attractiveness in marriage, there are a few other factors that contribute to a person's overall appearance. One of these factors is the use of makeup. Some women look great with no makeup at all, while others need a little help to showcase their best features. A makeup artist at a department store can offer advice, but your husband should be there to judge the result. After all, he's the person to impress. But while your objective is to meet his need for physical attractiveness, you should also like the change.

The same can be said of hairstyle—select one that is attractive to your spouse and comfortable for you. There are books at hair salons that illustrate a variety of hairstyles. Go through these books with your spouse, asking which style he or she finds most attractive. Then choose one that you both like as your next hairstyle.

When it comes to choosing clothes, dress to be attractive to each other. When buying clothes, ask for each other's honest feedback when trying a particular outfit. Husbands, remember that just because you think your ratty old college sweatshirt is the most comfortable piece of clothing on the planet doesn't mean you should wear it to dinner with your wife tonight. You may not care what you're wearing most of the time, but she probably does. And wives, pay as much, if not more, attention to your choice of pajamas as you do to what you wear in public each day. When you dress for bed, you're dressing strictly for your husband. Wearing a worn-out nightgown to bed because "nobody will see it" misses an important point: One very special and important person does see it, so why not wear something attractive?

How does your spouse feel about your physical appearance? Is there anything about your makeup, hair, or clothing they might like to see change? Remember: these cosmetic changes may be only skin-deep, but meeting your spouse's need for physical attractiveness will certainly deepen your love.

Day 5

A final factor we want to mention concerning physical attractiveness is personal hygiene. To be honest, we know few women but many men who have needed help with this problem.

You might ask your spouse the following questions: Would you like me to shower more frequently, particularly before bed? Do my clothes smell clean? Does my breath smell good? Do I stay on top of keeping my hair looking good and shaving regularly? There may be other areas of personal hygiene that your spouse wants you to address. Don't just let it go, allowing your appearance to create Love Bank withdrawals.

We've encountered many women who feel their primary obstacle to lovemaking has been their husband's lack of personal hygiene, especially at bedtime. Don't let that problem come between you. Getting into the habit of taking a shower and using mouthwash is usually all it takes to solve it once and for all.

Perhaps you are still unconvinced that physical attractiveness is a worthy objective. If so, consider what it means to be physically attractive. It simply means that your appearance makes someone feel good. You meet an emotional need by the way you look. If physical attractiveness meets an emotional need of your spouse, why ignore it? Why not deposit love units whenever you have a chance?

For some women, the prospect of becoming physically attractive seems completely out of reach. These women have fallen for the lie that some women are born attractive while others are not. We want to offer you a different perspective: attractiveness is what you do with what you have. Remember: in your marriage, it's your calling to look not only to your own interests but also to the interests of your spouse. So, for the sake of your spouse, your marriage, and your own health, be a good steward of the body God has given you.

PRAYER FOR THE WEEK

Lord, help us to honor you through how we treat our bodies. Help us to keep ourselves attractive for each other's pleasure and to stay healthy so we can serve one another and you. Help us not to become discouraged by challenges along the way, but give us perseverance and encouragement to see it through. And help us to create a lifestyle that makes the most of these bodies you have given us, for our delight and your glory.

Week 31

Financially Secure

By wisdom a house is built,
    and through understanding it is established;
through knowledge its rooms are filled
    with rare and beautiful treasures.

Proverbs 24:3–4

W hen I met Sean and Mindy, Sean's career had reached a plateau. He had advanced about as far as he could with that company. Mindy admitted privately that she had lost respect for Sean. "I suppose I shouldn't feel this way, but he can't earn enough to pay our bills, and now he wants me to go back to work to make up the difference. With the children so young, I just don't want to do that."

When I asked whether they could cut expenses, Mindy seemed desperate. "As far as I'm concerned we're at the bare minimum now. I suppose we couldn't afford a bigger house, but now we're into it.

We could never get along without a second car. We just live too far out to leave me home alone without some kind of transportation."

I could see that talking to Mindy about lowering her quality of life was pointless, so I made this suggestion: "Perhaps Sean could earn quite a bit more if he finished his education—he has two years left, right? Would you be willing to go to work to help him?"

"Well, I suppose I could—just so it wouldn't be forever," Mindy replied. "I'll talk to Sean and see what he thinks."

Within a few weeks Sean and Mindy had it worked out. She had found a full-time job, and his company had allowed him to take a part-time position so he could attend college and finish his degree.

Mindy was pleased to see Sean trying to improve his income-producing potential, and she did not mind the sacrifice because she knew it wouldn't be permanent. Ironically, Mindy loved her job so much that she continued working even after Sean had completed school and was earning enough to support her. In the end she gained respect for her husband and a valued career for herself.

— Day 1 —

Sean and Mindy were in a tough position: their income simply wasn't enough to cover their household expenses. When couples come to this realization, whether they're making a budget, considering job choices, or anything else that involves their finances, the bottom line is always the same: they must prioritize. But when it comes to setting financial priorities—deciding what is essential and what is discretionary—spouses often don't agree. And in the case of financial planning, couples face a serious complication: the wife usually has an emotional need for financial support.

Ask yourselves the question: "If I had known before we were married that my spouse would not be able to provide any financial support for our family, would I have gone through with the wedding?" Most men answer that question with a "yes." Most women answer "no," or at least, "I'd have to give it some thought." Granted, many wives will rise to the occasion and support the family if a husband becomes unable to work, or is laid off for an extended period of time. But it's very unusual for a wife to encourage her husband to let her earn the family income while he becomes a homemaker.

In truth, almost every woman marries a man for his money, or at least the money she expects him to earn during their lifetime together. Deep down, she needs him to earn enough to support their family. We refer to this as the emotional need for financial support, and it's much stronger than most couples think it is in our culture of dual-income families.

How would you feel if your spouse were unable to contribute financially to your household? You might be surprised to discover that you each have different answers to this question. Talk about it with each other. Does one of you have an emotional need for financial support?

Day 2

As we consider the emotional need of financial support this week, let's look for insight in Proverbs 24:3–4: "By wisdom a house is built, and through understanding it is established; through knowledge its rooms are filled with rare and beautiful treasures."

Have you and your spouse built your home on a foundation of wisdom? Your reverence for God is the beginning of wisdom (Prov. 9:10), and that wisdom provides you with the truth of the gospel and the reality of God's grace. Knowledge of God is understanding. Have you established your home by understanding? If you want to understand God's ways, and to understand your children and each other, your home will be established. And with your knowledge you fill it with all the things that make life "rare and beautiful."

Hebrews 13:5 also provides some wisdom about taking care of your family financially: "Keep your lives free from the love of money and be content with what you have." Sometimes, the love of money makes a couple their own worst enemies. They create a standard of living they cannot afford, which makes it impossible for the husband to fulfill his wife's need for financial support. Their marriage suffers unnecessary stress as they try to figure out how to pay for things they could actually do without.

Is your life characterized by a love of money, or by contentment with what you have? Spend time in prayer as a couple, asking for forgiveness if you have given money too high of a priority, especially if this has hurt your marriage. Ask the Lord to help you develop contentment with what you have.

––––––––––– **Day 3** –––––––––––

Some couples look on budgets as a "necessary evil," but we like to call a budget a "necessary good." Without a realistic budget, it's easy for a family's expenses to outpace the husband's income—which makes it impossible for him to fulfill his wife's need for financial support. To more fully understand the quality of life you can afford, we encourage you to make three budgets: one to describe what you need, one to describe what you want, and one to describe what you can afford.

We provide a form in the questionnaires section of marriagebuilders.com called the *Financial Support Inventory: Needs and Wants Budget*. You may copy it free of charge and use it to create these three budgets.

The *needs budget* should include the monthly cost of meeting the necessities of your life. We recommend that the wife determine what the household needs are, and how much money they require. Only the husband's income should be included in the needs budget. If his income is sufficient to meet all the family needs, by definition he's met his wife's need for financial support. Without this budget, his success in meeting this need may not be obvious to her.

The *wants budget* is to be completed by both spouses with both incomes included. This is basically a wish list for both of you, but avoid including items that are clearly out of your reach. It should contain everything in the needs budget plus expenses you would like to add to it.

The *affordable budget* is your final budget. After the needs budget is met, you use any remaining income to purchase wants you can both enthusiastically agree to buy. This is where your negotiating skills will pay off, because it will require wisdom, creativity, and empathy to know how to spend your limited resources.

You have been called to a life in which, by God's grace, you're not ruled by money. So take the time to make a budget that reflects your family's priorities, and then stick to this budget so that you manage well the resources God has given you.

Day 4

In my counseling experience, the affordable budget has triggered a question from many husbands: "Should I expect my wife to work to help us pay for the wants in our lives?" We think it should be up to her.

Wives usually want a choice between following a career and being a homemaker—or possibly they want a combination of the two. They often want to be homemakers in their younger years, while their children are small. Later, when the children have grown, they may want to develop careers outside the home. But the choice should be theirs. If they do choose a career, the money they earn should not have to be spent on basic needs. That gives them an option to stop working if they so desire. To put it all very simply, many families need to learn how to live on what a husband can earn.

You may be squirming at this point. The thought of lowering your standard of living is difficult for most couples. But if one of the wife's deep emotional needs is to have her husband support the family financially, then that family should live within the means provided by the husband's salary.

You may not feel this way. In fact, you may have discovered that neither of you has a need for financial support. If that's the case, when either one of you decides not to work, the other feels no resentment by being the sole breadwinner. But it's unusual to find such marriages, and it's more likely that your marriage fits our description.

Reflect on this command from Hebrews 13:5: "Keep your lives free from the love of money and be content with what you have." Then read Proverbs 24:3–4 again. Has the love of a certain kind of lifestyle been undermining the filling of your rooms with "rare and beautiful treasures"? Pray that the Lord would help you handle your finances in a way that honors him and enriches your marriage.

Day 5

Today we want to return to our opening example: Sean and Mindy. Their situation is prevalent in the wake of recent economic downturns. What happens when a husband's income is not sufficient to pay for needs budget expenses? We have met countless couples caught in this trap. He works as hard as he can, coming home tired every night. But his paycheck just won't go far enough. His wife faces the difficult choice of being unhappy while working to make up the difference or being unhappy while putting up with an intolerable quality of life. Her Love Bank is draining.

We sympathize with the man trapped in this situation. He does the best he can, yet cannot meet his wife's emotional need for financial support. Isn't there an answer to this kind of impasse? He could try to obtain a pay raise or make a job change that pays more—or he may need to go to the trouble of a career change.

When a husband's income is insufficient, we recommend that he do what Sean did: try to improve his job skills. While he is training for this new job, the family may temporarily lower its standard of living, his wife may go to work, or perhaps both adjustments will be made. We have found that, like Mindy, most women are willing to lower their quality of life and go to work to help support the family—if it is a temporary solution to a financial crisis. In fact, making this kind of temporary sacrifice can often prove to be a powerful builder of rapport and affection in a marriage. Couples have told us they are amazed at how satisfied they are living on a shoestring budget when both know they are working together to make a dream come true.

The bottom line is that it's possible to live on much less than we do. Almost any family can live comfortably on less than they presently spend. We simply want you to consider the idea that many people think they need things they may not really need. Don't let the cost of high living standards lead you to lose any of life's most valuable treasures—especially your marriage.

PRAYER FOR THE WEEK

Lord, we may have filled our lives with things we don't really need. Help us to use our money wisely by budgeting our spending to reflect your priorities for our life and marriage. Please deepen our contentment with what we have, for we are thankful for what you have given us. Help us to make the changes in our budget and spending habits that would give us greater fulfillment and would honor and glorify you. Help us to build our home with wisdom and understanding, and give us the knowledge we need to fill that home with what you know is best for us. Thank you for your living, faithful provision for us. Help us not take it for granted.

Week 32

Is a Man's Home His Castle?

Be devoted to one another in brotherly love. Honor one another above yourselves.

Romans 12:10

When Natalie was growing up, she loved playing house. While she eventually outgrew her dolls, she still enjoyed baking for her friends or making dinner for her family once in a while. And when she met Andy, she started to dream of making a perfect life for them.

But the realities of life with small children proved a daily challenge to Natalie's desire to keep the house clean or put creative dinners on the table. She found herself overwhelmed trying to keep up with her own expectations. Sometimes she wished she could just escape. Andy occasionally complained about the state of the house, but he didn't offer to help. He felt that as long as Natalie was a full-time homemaker, he should be able to take it easy after coming home from work. That left her feeling resentful.

Leslie and Jackson had a different story to tell. Leslie had taken three months for maternity leave when Erica was born, but had returned to work as soon as it ended. By the time she picked up Erica after work at six, fed her, and got her in bed, she barely had any energy left to hold a conversation, much less make dinner or do laundry. Leslie had hired someone to clean the house once a week, but many household tasks remained. Jackson was rarely home before seven and was very little help after that. They would usually order out, crash in front of the television, give Erica her late-night feeding, and go to bed, only to do it again the next day. Leslie knew few women who stayed home with their children, and she doubted they could live on her husband's income. But she was very tired most of the day, and also very resentful that Jackson wouldn't do his fair share of the household tasks.

Andy and Jackson both had a need for domestic support: a craving for their wives to manage household and childcare tasks. But neither wife was meeting that need to their satisfaction. One wife was trying, but was certainly not "cheerful" about it—and her ineffectiveness was growing. The other was so exhausted she simply couldn't do it.

Day 1

Over the past five decades a revolution in male attitudes regarding housework and childcare is supposed to have taken place, with men pitching in to take an equal share of the tasks. But this revolution has not necessarily changed their emotional needs. Many of the men I counsel still tell me in private that they need domestic support as much as ever. For them it is a basic emotional need.

How can you determine if you have this emotional need? Ask yourself this question: Would you marry someone who would never provide domestic support? Imagine that just prior to the wedding vows, your fiancé said, "When we marry and have children, I'll meet your other emotional needs, but don't expect me to cook meals, clean the house, or diaper the baby." In my experience with couples, if a man were to take this position, the woman would not be happy with it, but it wouldn't stop the wedding. On the other hand, if the woman were to say it, her man might call it off. Why? He has a need for domestic support. He needs his wife to manage the home.

Of course, it's up to you to discover your basic emotional needs, and you may find that this need simply isn't an issue for either of you. But what if your spouse does have this need? We'd encourage you to remember Philippians 2:3–5: you are to look not only to your own interests but also to the interests of others. If your husband needs domestic support, you need to take it seriously. How can you meet this need?

This may be a difficult question for you to answer. In past chapters, we have talked about making drastic changes—changing careers, moving, dropping activities—if your marriage is being undermined. Are you willing to make such changes in order to meet your spouse's need for domestic support? Be honest with each other as you think through the implications of these questions today.

—— Day 2 ——

Fifty years ago, it wasn't too difficult for the average wife to meet her husband's need for domestic support; she was a full-time home-maker. But things have changed. Today, the average wife is employed full-time, and the division of domestic responsibilities has become a major source of marital conflict. Not only is she unable to meet her husband's need for domestic support, but now she also senses that need. Men and women share the same fantasy: coming home to a clean house with the smell of dinner in the air and the children fed, bathed, and calm.

There is almost unanimous agreement today that both a husband and wife should share household responsibilities if they both work full-time. But the wife's instinct to care for the home and children, combined with the husband's need for domestic support, can easily get in the way of an enthusiastic agreement regarding domestic responsibilities. With the pressures they both face, how does the average dual-career couple come to a fair division of labor?

As we have mentioned earlier, when it comes to making any behavioral change, motivation is almost everything. If the change is enjoyable to the one who makes it, or if there is a reward for making the change, you can safely assume it will happen. But if the change is unpleasant, and if there is no reward for the effort, all the promises to change will ultimately be broken.

We'll offer you some practical steps for dividing household responsibilities in the days ahead. But before we do, we want you to let Romans 12:10 set the tone: "Be devoted to one another in brotherly love. Honor one another above yourselves." Do you honor your spouse above yourself? Are you devoted to him or her—even in meeting their need for domestic support?

Day 3

The plan we suggest to create a fair division of labor is very controversial. But it works. So even if your first reaction is negative, we strongly recommend you give it a chance to prove itself.

First, we recommend that you make a list of all of your household responsibilities, including childcare. As you make each entry on your list, briefly describe the responsibility. Then note which spouse wants the task accomplished (it may be both) and how important it is to each of you (use a scale from 0–5, with 0 indicating no importance and 5 indicating most important).

Second, make two new lists, one list titled "His Responsibilities" and the other titled "Her Responsibilities." Each of you should select tasks that you would enjoy doing, don't mind doing, or want to do yourself so they can be done a certain way. Cross each of these items off the original list and add them to one of the two new lists.

Now, what should you do with the tasks on your first list that neither of you wants to do? You might think it would make sense to divide these up equally, but we find this doesn't work in practice. Spouses aren't likely to follow through on chores they don't feel are important.

So the third step in dividing household tasks is to use motivational considerations to divide the list: assign responsibility to the person who gave it the highest importance rating.

At this point in our plan, most wives react with alarm. "I know how this will turn out," they complain. "All the remaining tasks will end up on my list. My husband could care less about keeping our home neat and clean." But telling your husband it's his responsibility to do something you want done isn't motivating. In fact, it's usually demotivating and is likely to lead to an argument, rather than giving you the help you desire. So for the sake of your marriage, add the items to your own list of responsibilities or assume that they won't get done.

Don't worry: we'll talk more about motivating your spouse's help with domestic chores tomorrow. But for today, go through the steps we've described to divide domestic responsibilities.

Day 4

Yesterday we presented a way to assign household responsibilities fairly. You divided them according to your willingness and desire to have them accomplished. But when a wife first sees her list of responsibilities, she usually feels overwhelmed—especially when we add the essential condition that she is to have eight hours of sleep every night. To address this situation, which is impossible for most women, we encourage wives to consider how they can shift some of the responsibility to hired help or to the children.

But there's another way for wives to get help—from their husbands. We believe it's possible to motivate a man, even one with a need for domestic support, to help his wife with household tasks.

There's hardly a wife who doesn't want help with domestic responsibilities, and she wants that help from her husband. But trying to force him to do them by being disrespectful or appealing to his guilt doesn't work because it's not motivational. What will motivate him? We recommend that she *appreciate his help*.

But before she can sincerely appreciate what he does, she must assume responsibility for doing it. If she thinks some chores are his responsibility, then when he completes them he's simply done his duty. But if she accepts those chores as her responsibility—part of meeting her husband's deep emotional need for domestic support—then she will be truly grateful for assistance, and he will deposit units in her Love Bank when he offers to help.

You already have one number assigned to each task—the importance of the task to each of you. But the fourth step in a fair division of labor requires that you write a number from 0 to 5 on each other's list of responsibilities indicating how many love units you think would be deposited if your spouse were to help you or do that task for you (0 means you would experience no pleasure; 5 indicates you would experience maximum pleasure and would be eternally grateful).

If these ratings are accurate, it means that whenever you have helped your spouse with a task that was rated a 4 or 5, you will be depositing many love units. Your help will make your spouse happy and it will be appreciated. Share your answers with each other.

Day 5

We hope you took the time to complete yesterday's assignment. If you did, you now have some great ideas for showing love to your spouse. If cooking dinner or ironing shirts makes Love Bank deposits, why not do those things? If picking up socks will gain your spouse's genuine appreciation, why would anyone resist doing it? It is not only an act of care, but of wisdom. By doing for each other what your spouse appreciates most, you will have the feeling of love throughout your entire lives.

Your spouse's response to your help will prove whether or not love units are being deposited. If your spouse thanks you when you perform the task and expresses his or her appreciation with affection and admiration, you know you are on the right track. But if your spouse doesn't seem to notice your help, next time try helping with a different task.

As you look for these opportunities to fill your spouse's Love Bank, make sure you are not making withdrawals from your own Love Bank. If you suffer in an effort to help your spouse with a household task, you will never get into the habit of helping with that task. And deposits in your spouse's Love Bank will be offset by withdrawals in yours. Remember, when you decide to help your spouse with one of his or her responsibilities, it does not make it your responsibility. Only when help with a task is seen as a gift—as an act of care—does it have the maximum impact on the Love Bank.

We think our approach to dividing household responsibilities will help you keep your Love Banks full. It gives you a way to show mutual care, especially when you feel like being uncaring. And it prevents you from forcing your spouse into an unpleasant way of life. Remember: you are called to "Be devoted to one another in brotherly love. Honor one another above yourselves" (Rom. 12:10). The daily demand of maintaining your home and caring for your children provide ample opportunities to show your devotion and to honor one another. Take advantage of those opportunities to help your spouse and you will enjoy a lifetime of love in your home.

⟶⟶ PRAYER FOR THE WEEK ⟵⟵

Lord, please help us to show our care for each other in the way we share domestic responsibilities. Help us to understand what you value in our home, and how we should prioritize our tasks. Please give us sensitivity toward one another, so that we can help each other, not reluctantly or out of compulsion, but from our heart with a cheerful spirit.

Week 33

Train a Child—Together

Train a child in the way he should go,
and when he is old he will not turn from it.

Proverbs 22:6

Jacob and Amanda had been dating for several months when they started to talk about getting married one day. Amanda raised the subject of having children, and Jacob was enthusiastic. She was delighted, and began to picture him as the perfect family man.

Shortly thereafter they were married, and in a few years they had two children. Jacob had been excited about the idea of having the kids, and showed them affection when he held them. But it quickly became apparent that he didn't have a good grasp of what his role was as their father. His own father had left the parenting to his mom and had remained at the perimeter of their family life; he was usually in the other room watching TV. Jacob had few memories of playing catch with his dad in the yard or going out for any kind of father-son time. It was his mom who went to all his games.

Jacob had made church attendance a priority for his family because he felt his children would learn moral values there. But one Sunday the pastor began talking about a father's role in the family. Jacob's ears perked up. It was as if the pastor was talking right to him. "Fathers, are you making an intentional effort to guide your children in the ways you want them to go? Proverbs 22:6 tells us to 'Train a child in the way he should go, and when he is old he will not turn from it.' Are you taking an active role in training your children?" *No*, Jacob admitted to himself. He knew that he made an effort to play with the kids sometimes, but that was about it. Little thought went into their training. He had thought his wife and the church would take care of that.

The pastor continued. "Men and women, God is very clear about what he wants you to do with your children. He wants you to teach them. He wants you to train them. And it is going to take thought, effort, and being on the same page. One of the most important passages to the people of Israel was found in Deuteronomy 6:4–7. It reads, 'Hear, O Israel: The LORD our God, the LORD is one. Love the LORD your God with all your heart and with all your soul and with all your strength. These commandments that I give you today are to be upon your hearts. Impress them on your children. Talk about them when you sit at home and when you walk along the road, when you lie down and when you get up.' Are the commands of God on your hearts? Are you impressing them on your children? Are you talking about God and his plans and purposes and commands when you're in the car, or sitting at home, or going for a walk—at bedtime, at breakfast? Is your family life centered on God and his purposes for your family?"

Jacob's head was spinning. He knew he wanted to have a role in his children's lives, but until that moment he wasn't sure what the purpose would be. Now he had a focus: he needed to train his children in God's ways. He needed to understand God's ways himself and then teach his children how to follow them. That would take quite a bit of time and effort. It sounded overwhelming, but also very important.

Amanda cast a sideways glance at Jacob. He smiled at her, and tears came to her eyes. She could tell that something was changing. *God, are you answering my prayers?* she wondered.

Day 1

Like Amanda, most women experience a basic emotional need for family commitment. A wife wants her husband to teach their children the most important values in life and to set an example for them to follow so they grow up to be like him. Her need for family commitment is met when a husband commits himself to the moral and educational development of their children.

Women seem to know instinctively what psychologists have discovered in research and practice: a father has a profound influence on his children. Our fathers exerted a powerful influence on our development. They may not have known it at the time, because we often disagreed with them. But upon reaching adulthood, we found ourselves following their lead. This development of our own moral values was extremely important to our mothers, and we are both certain they gave their husbands a great deal of credit for training us up in the way they wanted us to go.

Jacob felt challenged to increase his family commitment when his pastor preached about Deuteronomy 6:4–7. When you read this passage, what is *your* first response? Does it seem excessive? Impossible? Irrelevant? For some, this passage seems to hold up an unreachable standard. And if it's simply a list of topics for conversation, it might indeed be difficult. But it is much more than that. God wants parents to follow his commands and "impress them on the hearts" of their children. This is vital to a child's spiritual development. But for many husbands, it's also a significant way to meet his wife's emotional need for family commitment.

Wife, in what ways does your husband's investment in your children affect your feelings toward him? Is it an emotional need for you? Share your thoughts and feelings on this subject with him.

— Day 2 —

As a person who has been saved by Christ, you have been given the gift of the Holy Spirit. And, as Paul says in 1 Corinthians 2, the purpose of this gift is "that we may understand what God has freely given us" (v. 12). He goes on to explain:

> The man without the Spirit does not accept the things that come from the Spirit of God, for they are foolishness to him, and he cannot understand them, because they are spiritually discerned. . . . But we have the mind of Christ. (1 Cor. 2:14, 16)

The Holy Spirit reveals the mind of Christ to you. And one of God's main purposes for your parenting is that you share this mind of Christ with your children. God wants your life to be framed by the gift of his grace, and for you to freely communicate this gift to your children. If you are training your children in the way they should go and showing them the love of Christ in all of the circumstances they face, then you are fulfilling your duty to them.

Training involves conversation, a life in which parents and children are continually interacting. The father is available to his children—not only to instruct, but to listen, to walk alongside them, to play. But training goes beyond conversation. Your children will watch you carefully to see if you practice what you preach. If you want them to consider the interests of others to be as important as their own interests (Phil. 2:4), are you following your own advice, especially toward your spouse? If you want them to live in constant contact with the Spirit of God for guidance (1 Thess. 5:17), do they see you seeking God's will throughout the day?

Read Deuteronomy 6:4–7 together and think back over the past week. Have you been training your children according to God's Word?

Day 3

In previous weeks, we have emphasized the importance of establishing priorities. What are your most important goals in life? We also made the observation that your schedule will determine what you will actually accomplish in a week—if it's not on your schedule, it probably won't be done.

Therefore, we encouraged you to establish a specific time each week when you would both sit down together with your weekly calendar and plan the week's events with your priorities in mind. The priority we wanted you to place at the top of your list was your care for each other. We recommended you devote fifteen hours each week to meeting each other's intimate emotional needs and building a great marriage.

But there's another goal that takes consistent scheduling to achieve— the goal of "bringing up your children in the way they should go." As with the time you set aside for undivided attention, we also suggest setting aside time for what we call *quality family time*. This is not to be confused with childcare tasks—feeding, clothing, and watching over children to keep them safe. Those are domestic tasks, which we discussed last week. Quality family time is when the family is together for the purpose of teaching the children life's most important values.

Have you made family time a priority in your relationship? What does quality family time currently look like for you? Pray about this together today, asking God to show you if there are ways you could improve your time together as a family.

Day 4

Yesterday, we challenged you to make family time a priority in your relationship. But how much quality family time is sufficient to influence your children and train them to become successful adults? We've studied that question and have come to the conclusion that it takes about the same amount of time as it takes to stay in love—fifteen hours a week. If you schedule fifteen hours a week to be together as a family, teaching your children the most important values, you will tend to have more influence on their character than anything or anyone else, including their peers.

Without a doubt, the hours spent with your children are some of the most important hours of the week. But if you are already devoting fifteen hours each week to your spouse, do you actually have time for family left in your schedule? You probably don't have much "extra time" right now, so if you want to prioritize your marriage and family, you likely need to eliminate other scheduled events that are not as important. It's hard to give up activities that have been part of your lives for quite a while. But are they more important than your care for each other and your care for your children?

Remember, a time budget (your weekly schedule) is like a financial budget. It helps keep your priorities straight. If you don't budget your money, you will make so many low priority purchases you'll have no money left for things that are truly important to you. The same is true with your time. If you don't schedule your week with your highest priorities in mind, you'll run out of time before you can accomplish them.

Take a look at your weekly schedule. Do you currently include fifteen hours for quality family time each week? If not, what would you have to eliminate to make your family time a priority?

Day 5

Yesterday, we encouraged you to carve out fifteen hours each week for quality family time. So what should you actually do with those hours? The purpose of quality family time is to *train your children in the way they should go.* Make sure your entire family is together when you do it so that you develop a cooperative spirit. Make it a time for fun with your children, not a time of drudgery. Your time could include game nights, bike rides, reading to your children before bedtime, helping the children with homework, and getting everyone involved in family projects.

Make the most of the opportunities in your daily schedule. If your family currently has meals on the run, grabbing a bite to eat separately, start having your meals together. When you eat, take a few moments to read a Bible passage and discuss it. Then pray together. See if your children have any prayer requests on their young hearts. And instead of activities that separate your family members, try to find things you can do together. One of the biggest consumers of parental time is sports leagues. If they prevent you from being together as a family, are they worth it?

Children are easier to influence than teens or adults. So if your children are still young, make the most of your ability to mold them with quality moral standards. If you take family time seriously in their early growth stages, you will reap the benefits throughout your life together as a family. If they are already in their teens, you may need to be more creative and devote some additional budget toward teen-friendly activities you can do together.

Whatever stage of life your family is in, keep in mind the goal of training your child "in the way he should go." As you spend this time building a strong family, you'll also be meeting your spouse's need for family commitment and strengthening your love.

PRAYER FOR THE WEEK

Lord, we want to train our children to follow your ways. We want them to know you as we have come to know you. Help us to give our children the quality time necessary to train them in the way they are to go. We don't want to lose the opportunity you have given us to draw our children closer to you. Thank you for providing this family for us to enjoy. Help us to care for them faithfully.

Week 34

Parenting in Unity

Fathers, do not exasperate your children; instead, bring them up
in the training and instruction of the Lord.

Ephesians 6:4

Last week, we met Jacob and Amanda at a strategic point in
their relationship. Though Jacob had been an affectionate
father to his children, he hadn't taken his parenting responsibilities seriously, leaving Amanda alone in her efforts to instruct
and discipline them. Frustrated by his lack of involvement with the
kids, Amanda felt her respect and love for Jacob slowly start to wane.

Fortunately, God intervened with a powerful sermon one Sunday
morning. Listening to the pastor's challenging words concerning
parenting, Jacob recognized his mistake in leaving all the childrearing responsibilities up to Amanda. He felt a new desire to invest in
his children's development, but he had no idea where to start. Jacob
realized he needed training, and he was open to reading some books

their pastor suggested. He and Amanda also attended a parenting seminar that showed them ways to improve communication with their children.

When Jacob began to understand the privilege of raising his children to know Christ, he knew that the time spent and the training required would be worth the effort. He started making a concentrated effort to train their children, and to talk about God's plans and purposes in the course of daily life.

But Jacob didn't anticipate the significant impact it would have on his relationship with Amanda. He soon realized that his parenting efforts were not just an investment in his children. They were an investment in his marriage as well. When he started to apply his newfound parenting skills, her respect for him went through the roof and her love for him gained a new sparkle. She had been praying that Jacob would take on this role in their family, and when she saw him doing what she needed him to do, it made her love him all the more. She no longer felt alone in parenting responsibilities. Instead, she and Jacob had become the best kind of parenting team—a mom and dad in love.

Day 1

We want to devote a second week to one of the greatest challenges—and rewards—of marriage: training your children. Caring for your spouse in the midst of a bustling family life may be one of the biggest tests of your relationship. But if you are devoted to building a strong marriage, you will not only provide the stable home that kids crave, but also ensure that you create a united and consistent approach to child training.

Do you remember reading Deuteronomy 6:4–7 last week? It says:

Hear, O Israel: The LORD our God, the LORD is one. Love the LORD your God with all your heart and with all your soul and with all your strength. These commandments that I give you today are to be upon your hearts. Impress them on your children. Talk about them when you sit at home and when you walk along the road, when you lie down and when you get up.

Parents have a vital role in the lives of their children, and God expects them to take their role as instructors seriously.

Parent-instruction manuals, books, and courses abound, with information on everything from toilet training to enforcing curfew. But underlying all of the methods and ideas for childrearing is one basic fact: mothers and fathers must parent in unity. If you and your spouse are not of one mind when it comes to raising your children, then you will not only confuse your children, you will also make sizable withdrawals from your Love Banks. But if you work together to find a parenting style you agree to with enthusiasm, it will make you effective teachers while also building your Love Banks balances.

Start this week by discussing these questions: What are the key truths about who God is and what Christ has done that you want to communicate to your children? In what ways should you be communicating these truths to your children?

Day 2

In family after family, we have witnessed children that manipulate and drive a wedge between their parents. Father favors Mary; Mother favors Joan. So Mary goes to Father for money, and he tries to give it to her without Mother knowing. When Joan finds out about it, she demands the same treatment. Mother tries to make Father give Joan the same amount of money, resulting in a big conflict between husband and wife. To avoid this kind of scenario, we encourage you to remember that *all* of your decisions must result from mutual agreement—including your parenting decisions. If you cannot agree, take no action.

From an emotional needs standpoint, it makes no sense for a father to ignore his wife's opinions regarding childrearing. If he wants to meet her need for family commitment, she needs him to join her in the educational and moral development of their children—not take over completely. But it also makes no sense for him to do it her way when they don't agree. He won't be an effective parent if he goes about it "reluctantly or under compulsion" (2 Cor. 9:7). At best, his training will lack vigor, and at worst he will sabotage his wife's efforts.

Wise parents will negotiate with each other until they have mutually enthusiastic agreement about their childrearing choices. When a mother and father agree on the rules their children will be expected to follow and how they will discipline misbehavior, they avoid the common mistakes made by most parents. Children are less likely to challenge your decisions when they know you made them together. And if one spouse has a need for family commitment, this approach also helps fulfill that need.

Do you agree on the rules and discipline methods used in your home—or do your parenting strategies go in different directions? What kind of family rules can you both agree to with enthusiasm?

Day 3

Yesterday, we explained how important it is for you and your spouse to negotiate together regarding childrearing. Today we encourage you to think about how you will interpret those family rules for your children in a way they can understand. Children need to understand why they should do this or that.

Sometimes parents play the "because I said so" card because it usually gets the job done—children do what they're told. But parents lose an opportunity to teach moral, ethical, and personal values when they do that. Ephesians 6:4 commands, "Fathers, do not exasperate your children; instead, bring them up in the training and instruction of the Lord." You're far less likely to frustrate your children if you train and instruct them in ways that make sense to them. So explain the values behind your rules. This is an essential aspect of your role as a godly and helpful parent.

Once your children understand the rules, be consistent in upholding them. Children don't take long to discover that rules may depend on Mom or Dad's mood. When Mom feels happy, they can do almost anything: run around the house, throw things, jump on the beds, and have a squirt-gun fight. When Dad comes home grumpy—watch out! Movement of any kind will be met with an angry outburst. If rules are applied inconsistently, their meaning is lost to children. Instead of teaching them a moral principle, you are making your mood the focus of their attention. So be a strong parenting team who sticks to the rules, regardless of your mood.

Could your children be feeling "exasperated" by any rules that are unclear or inconsistent in your home? How could you work together to do a better job of explaining and sticking to the rules you've agreed to for your family?

Day 4

We might long for angelic children who listen to our every word, but in reality, our "cherubs" often stick their fist in the cookie jar or use it to beat on their sister. What do you do as parents when your children insist on breaking the rules? The bottom line is that you must learn to punish your children properly. Some parents will cringe at the very idea of punishment; they believe firmly in providing only positive reinforcement. But we read in Proverbs 13:24, "He who spares the rod hates his son, but he who loves him is careful to discipline him." A loving parent will provide consistent, careful discipline.

The way you punish your children should depend on their age. We have observed that children whose parents never spank them often run wild. But corporal punishment should be used only in the early years (no later than age seven), and should always be used to send a message—never to inflict physical injury. The word "rod" used in

231

Proverbs should be read "punishment," but not "a physical beating with a stick." A spanking given without anger and followed by prayer together can get the point across when children are very young.

But when children are between the ages of eight and twelve, noncorporal punishment is more appropriate and far more effective. Taking away privileges is a time-honored way for parents to punish older children. Incentives for good behavior should begin to replace punishment for bad behavior when training this age group. And as a child goes through the teenage years, we have found that punishment should be completely phased out in favor of incentives.

Do you both agree with the discipline strategies being used in your home? Are you satisfied with their effectiveness at promoting good behavior? Take some time today to discuss these issues with each other.

––––––––––––––––––– **Day 5** –––––––––––––––––––

All too often, parents discipline their children in a state of anger. Just the other day, I witnessed an example of such behavior in a shopping center parking lot. Inside the store, a child had been kicking and screaming because his mother would not buy him a toy. The ruckus continued through the checkout line, and all the way to their car. But after the mother had left the watchful eyes of guards and surveillance cameras, she began beating her son mercilessly. She wanted to let him know what a big mistake he'd made, and I'm sure he got the message.

As all parents know, it's tempting to let loose when communicating your displeasure. But discipline accompanied with anger doesn't usually work. It's impulsive, and it teaches a child that an angry outburst is an appropriate way to vent frustration. So control your anger before you discipline your children. By separating your emotion from the disciplinary action, you will become a far more effective disciplinarian.

Remember, the very best way to train your children is by example. So don't let them see parents who fly off the handle because of misbehavior, or who constantly bicker and undermine each other's discipline techniques. Instead, create a picture of calm and loving parents who work as a team to address inappropriate behavior.

As they grow, your children will notice far more than just your rules and punishments. When you demonstrate your care for each other by meeting each other's basic needs, and by protecting each other from your selfish habits, your children will learn what it means to be thoughtful. The quality family time you spend with your children, teaching them important values and a cooperative spirit, will go a long way toward creating children who need little or no punishment. And a childhood spent with parents who continually demonstrate the grace of Christ in the family will have immeasurable influence on your children when they become adults.

PRAYER FOR THE WEEK

Lord, we want to train our children faithfully and to integrate our relationship with you into our daily family life. Thank you for drawing us to the truth of your gospel; let it define our family relationships. Help each of us to fulfill the role you have given us in the instruction and training of our children. Enable us to labor together in this incredible work you have laid out for us to do. Let us trust you with our children, seeking your guidance at each step. Thank you for your love for our family.

Week 35

Loving Equals Admiring

Let the wife see that she respects and reverences her husband
[that she notices him, regards him, honors him, prefers him,
venerates, and esteems him; and that she defers to him, praises
him, and loves and admires him exceedingly].

Ephesians 5:33 AMP

When they were dating, Debbie couldn't stop talking about how wonderful Bob was. He had a great voice, and her heart raced when she heard him sing. He was well-read, and could make any author seem interesting. After a few months of dating, he came over and fixed her sink for her, saving her money and aggravation. She was head-over-heels in love. He could do anything. Her friends and family just laughed when they heard her talk about him; in her book, he was just about perfect.

Bob loved all of the attention and admiration Debbie heaped on him at every turn. It was something he was very unaccustomed to hearing because he had grown up with parents who had high expectations and offered little praise. If you excelled, you were doing what was expected of you. If you missed the mark, you heard about it. But Debbie was a source of consistent encouragement to Bob, and thought his many gifts and skills were extraordinary. When he asked her to marry him, she was overjoyed—she hit the jackpot!

Fast-forward twelve years. Bob was working as an accountant, a job that paid enough to allow Debbie to become a full-time mom to their three high-energy children. But motherhood had been an unexpected challenge for her; being home every day with rambunctious kids did not come naturally for Debbie, and she was drained from the demands of raising children. Their happiness and well-being had become the chief focus of her attention, leaving her little energy for Bob.

Before they had children, Debbie had been very proud of everything Bob did. But now, when he was asked to sing for church or tried to explain a good book he was reading, she seemed annoyed rather than proud. Those things were not important to her anymore.

Bob reacted to Debbie's lack of interest in him by burying himself in his work. He left for his office early, and came home late. Weekends were often spent working. She resented the way he was abandoning her and his family. But whenever she raised the issue, he explained it was the cost of giving her the freedom to be a full-time mom.

Debbie had met Bob's need for admiration very well while they were dating, but her admiration had evaporated after their children arrived. Their romantic love for each other had disappeared and the future of their marriage was at risk.

Day 1

Like Bob, most men find that honest admiration is a great motivator. When a woman tells a man she thinks he's wonderful, it inspires him to achieve more. He sees himself as being capable of handling new responsibilities and perfecting skills far above those of his present level. That inspiration helps him to take on some of the toughest responsibilities of life.

Admiration not only motivates; it also rewards the husband's existing achievements. When his wife tells him she appreciates him for what he has done, it gives him more satisfaction than he receives from his paycheck. And for some men—those with more fragile self-images—admiration also helps them believe in themselves. They are able to face their shortcomings with less defensiveness.

A man expects—and needs—his wife to be his most enthusiastic fan. He draws energy from her support and can usually achieve far more with her encouragement. You've heard the saying, "Behind every great man is a great woman." We'd like to amend it: *behind every man should be an admiring wife.* Men need admiring wives. Have you ever met a man whose wife is really good at showing him consistent admiration, love, respect, and encouragement? That man stands about a foot taller! When she meets that need, it has a very positive impact on his entire outlook.

Husband, do you feel admiration from your wife? What does her admiration mean to you? Is it an emotional need for you? Do you crave it? Do you feel great when you have it, and frustrated when you don't? Share your thoughts and feelings on this subject with your wife.

Day 2

In Ephesians 5:33, we find Scripture encouraging wives to meet their husband's need for admiration:

> Let the wife see that she respects and reverences her husband [that she notices him, regards him, honors him, prefers him, venerates, and esteems him; and that she defers to him, praises him, and loves and admires him exceedingly]." (Eph. 5:33 AMP)

We quoted from the Amplified Bible here because it gives you a sense of the full meaning of "respect"—it's a packed word! Paul calls wives to show their husbands a full-orbed respect.

Given most men's deep need for admiration, we think you can understand why criticism does so much damage in marriage. A husband wants his wife to be president of his fan club, not his worst critic. But some women feel it's their obligation to "straighten out" their husbands. Instead of showering her husband with accolades, she batters him with disapproval, resulting in huge Love Bank withdrawals.

Of course, we are not saying wives should keep complaints to themselves. In fact, we encourage complaints. It's the best way to get marital problems out into the open so they can be solved. But as we mentioned earlier, there's a distinction between complaints and criticisms. A wife might make a complaint, saying, "I feel lonely, and I'd like you to talk with me more often." But a critical wife adds disrespectful judgments to her complaint, saying, "You don't even care about me. I don't know why you ever wanted to get married if you were going to keep to yourself all the time." Which expression do you think will succeed? One places the problem on the docket for discussion and negotiation. The other belittles the husband and sets the stage for a fight.

When you have marital concerns in your marriage, do you tend to voice them as criticisms or complaints? Ask your husband this question today: "Do you feel that I tend to complain or tend to criticize when I have a problem with you?" Another question you might ask is, "Do you feel that I spend more time admiring you or criticizing you?"

Of course, the need for admiration is not found only in men. So, husband, you should ask your wife the same questions. Does she need your admiration?

Day 3

Before you start heaping words of praise on your spouse, we must give you a word of caution: never fake your admiration. By simply saying flattering words to each other, you can do more harm than good. To have any value, praise must genuinely reflect your feelings.

We can hear wives saying to themselves, *But what if my husband is a constant source of irritation? What if he always fouls things up? How can I learn to admire a man like that?* Sometimes a marriage can be so unsuccessful that spouses stop looking for the value in it. They want to get away from it so badly they convince themselves there is nothing to respect in each other. But that's an illusion. The truth is, regardless of the struggles you might be facing, there is value in everyone, even your spouse.

We encourage the wife of a man with a need for admiration to start looking for value in him. As she thinks of his characteristics and what he does, she begins to find things she genuinely admires about him. Writing them down as they occur to her helps her remember them and reflect on their value. It doesn't take long before she can express her honest admiration for some of her husband's strengths.

Tomorrow, we want to share some ideas that will give a wife more to admire about her husband. For today, though, spend some time in prayer, asking God to give you a deeper appreciation for your husband or wife—and then share words of admiration with each other.

Day 4

Many of us long to be admired by our spouse. But how can we build that admiration? As a husband learns to meet his wife's emotional needs, she finds herself responding with a natural and overflowing respect for him. She is able to express her admiration of him from the heart, which meets his need. Conversely, if a man does not meet her needs, she cannot in all honesty express the degree of admiration he needs from her.

Keeping this observation in mind, we have a simple plan to create genuine admiration in your marriage. First, we encourage spouses to make two lists. One list should describe behaviors you would admire in your spouse, and the other list should describe behaviors that destroy your admiration. It helps to list these behaviors in the categories of your most important needs (affection, family commitment, conversation, etc.). Second, read through each other's lists and make a trade, agreeing to work on some of the items identified by your spouse. Finally, create a plan to build new habits that will enhance your spouse's admiration. We find it's especially important to create incentives for repeating your new habits and disincentives for falling back into your old habits.

Here's how it worked for Bob and Debbie. When they made their lists, she said that his lack of interest in the children's activities destroyed her admiration for him. Together, Bob and Debbie created an incentive for Bob to practice a new habit. She would watch "Monday Night Football" with him any week in which he spent five hours with the children's activities; if he failed to do so, he would not watch any sports on television that week. They agreed to try the plan for five months, and although there was a slip-up along the way, the habit seemed ingrained by the end of their trial. Not only did Bob now spend five hours with the children, he had begun to plan new activities with them as well. Debbie found herself admiring Bob once again.

Are there any new habits you could build to create more admiration from your spouse? Discuss this question today. And remember, mere commitment won't get the job done if it's not accompanied by solid incentives to practice the new behavior for a good length of time.

Day 5

Yesterday, we saw how Debbie began to admire Bob again. Once those feelings of admiration returned, I coached her on what to do next: tell him! That obvious answer is not always as easy as it seems. Debbie had lost the habit of telling her husband she admired him. You may relate to this: just because you *feel* pride or admiration does not mean you *communicate* it very often.

Teach yourself to speak those words of praise, just as you have learned any other habit. At first it may seem awkward, but as your habit develops it will become smoother and more spontaneous. Then you'll have achieved your goal: the natural admiration he's always wanted from you.

Sometimes a woman fears expressing praise too soon, feeling that her husband might stop working on behavior that has not yet become habitual. But I advise her to communicate praise as soon as she feels even a *little* admiration—not just as a reward for change, but as a true expression of her feelings.

Remember, most men really *need* admiration. They thrive on it. So, wives, take the time to reflect on Ephesians 5:33. Think and pray about the specific ways you can communicate your admiration for your husband. Pay attention to the things that are important to him, and be intentional about communicating your admiration in ways that will matter to him. Ask the Lord to give you sensitivity to your husband, and pray for him in his endeavor to meet your needs. Be consistent and generous in your expressions of admiration, knowing it will build your husband's confidence and will also build your marriage.

PRAYER FOR THE WEEK

For the wife:

Lord, help me to admire my husband, to see those things he does that put me first, to notice when he meets my needs. Help me to support and care for my husband more deeply every day, and help me to encourage him in the way I talk to him.

For the husband:

Lord, help me to meet my wife's emotional needs in ways that encourage her admiration, and help me not to undermine it by doing things that disappoint her. Please give me greater sensitivity to her feelings and reactions to what I do, so that I will be a consistent encouragement to her.

Together:

Thank you for our marriage and for bringing us together; help us to be faithful in building it for your honor and glory.

Week 36

Love for a Lifetime

We have not received the spirit of the world but the Spirit who is from God, that we may understand what God has freely given us. This is what we speak, not in words taught us by human wisdom but in words taught by the Spirit, expressing spiritual truths in spiritual words. The man without the Spirit does not accept the things that come from the Spirit of God, for they are foolishness to him, and he cannot understand them, because they are spiritually discerned. The spiritual man makes judgments about all things, but he himself is not subject to any man's judgment:
> "For who has known the mind of the Lord that he may instruct him?"

But we have the mind of Christ.

1 Corinthians 2:12–16

We have started almost every week with a story. You've read about dozens of married couples, each with unique struggles and each with unique ways of overcoming them. Some of them fought. Others were barely speaking. Some of them felt exasperated with their spouse. Others felt nothing at all.

242

But over time, they were all able to reignite their love as they cared for each other's basic emotional needs.

This week, we encourage you to think about *your* story. Where has God taken you through the journey of marriage? If you were to write a brief description of how you met, what you expected of each other, and how your marriage actually turned out, how would it read?

It is our prayer that you have been challenged and encouraged by the experiences of other couples, particularly in the way they overcame what appeared to be insurmountable obstacles. As you have talked, shared, read, and thought through issues that all married couples should address, we hope you have found many tools to help you build a strong, Christ-centered marriage, one that is full of joy.

As we conclude our time together, we want you to reflect on the ways you've grown over the past thirty-five weeks. As you read these final thoughts, we hope you use this opportunity to discuss how God has been blessing your marriage.

——— Day 1 ———

When you think about your marriage, what would you say is the foundational biblical principle from which everything else flows? We have given that question quite a bit of thought, and have come to the conclusion that Genesis 2:24 is the starting point. When you married, two became one. "For this reason a man will leave his father and mother and be united to his wife, and they will become one flesh." You and your spouse are now one; this is the most basic assumption of marriage.

Christ affirms and clarifies this idea in the New Testament. Quoting Genesis 2:24, Jesus says, "So they are no longer two, but one. Therefore what God has joined together, let man not separate" (Matt. 19:6). In this bold statement, Christ leaves no doubt as to the meaning of "one flesh." They are to blend with each other.

Before you started this study, were there any areas where you were having difficulty "blending"? Were there any areas of independence where you were failing to live as one? We hope you have learned some valuable tools for blending with grace and care. What have been the most important insights you have taken away from your study of this book? Skim the chapters if you need to refresh your memory, and spend time sharing your responses with each other today.

Day 2

Throughout this book, we have described what it means to blend. We challenged you with the Policy of Joint Agreement, encouraging you to *never do anything without an enthusiastic agreement between you and your spouse*. You learned how to negotiate until reaching a solution that blends your attitudes, reactions, opinions, and beliefs. And you learned that neither of you should try to force your way of thinking on the other because that would not lead to a blended outcome.

We also introduced the Policy of Radical Honesty: *reveal to your spouse as much information about yourself as you know—your thoughts, feelings, habits, likes, dislikes, past history, daily activities, and future plans.* You were encouraged to discover your spouse's thoughts and to understand them. We asked you to spend time communicating honestly with each other so you would have all of the information you need to know when searching for mutually enthusiastic agreements. This policy was designed to help you find empathy for your spouse, knowing how your behaviors and habits affect him or her. When you know the mind of your spouse, you can develop true unity in your marriage.

Both the Policy of Joint Agreement and the Policy of Radical Honesty help you blend into true unity in marriage, despite your differences. Underlying these policies is an essential biblical principle:

> Do nothing out of selfish ambition or vain conceit, but in humility consider others better than yourselves. Each of you should look not

only to your own interests, but also to the interests of others. Your attitude should be the same as that of Christ Jesus. (Phil. 2:3–5)

We are not focused only on what we want out of life—we are to actively pursue our spouse's best interests too.

Have you been practicing the Policy of Joint Agreement and the Policy of Radical Honesty in your marriage? How have these concepts helped you discover each other's best interests? How have they helped you develop greater unity as a couple?

Day 3

In our devotional study, we spent several weeks describing what it means to care for each other in marriage. Caring love is expressed by meeting each other's most important emotional needs, and avoiding anything that would hurt each other.

You are each in a unique position to make each other happy. You give each other the exclusive right, and responsibility, to care for each other in ways that bring out the best in you—the feeling of romantic love for each other. This is achieved by meeting basic emotional needs: affection, sexual fulfillment, intimate conversation, recreational companionship, honesty and openness, physical attractiveness, financial support, domestic support, family commitment, and admiration. When you meet these needs for each other, you make each other feel fulfilled and loved.

But you are also in a unique position to make each other miserable. You can behave like a bull in a china shop. The negative effect of demands, disrespect, anger, dishonesty, annoying habits, and independent behavior are greatly magnified in marriage. When these Love Busters are allowed to exist, instead of feeling romantic love toward each other, you feel revulsion.

In past weeks, did you identify any Love Busters that needed to be overcome? What have you been doing to overcome them—and how has your decision to eliminate them affected your marriage? And what about your emotional needs? Have you both noticed any difference in your relationship since you've learned to meet them for each other?

Your care for each other is a calling that comes directly from God. Remind yourselves continually that you have married someone who is a cherished, beloved child of God, bought with a price. You are privileged to help each other know you have been forgiven in Christ and set free to live according to God's great plans.

Day 4

Why does God place such a high value on marriage? Why does he want marriage to be exclusive? It's because our marriage is a representation of our relationship with God himself. He wants us to know him in the same way that we know each other. He wants us to be faithful to each other, the same way we are to be faithful to him.

Over the past weeks, have you developed a deeper appreciation for God's perspective on your marriage? What have you been able to learn about your personal relationship with God as you've been working at building your marriage relationship?

We consider marriage to be a sacred union because of the many analogies in Scripture that compare marriage to our relationship with God. We are to know each other's minds just as we are to know the mind of Christ. How can we know the mind of Christ if we don't look for it through prayer and the study of his Word? Scripture is God's communication and revelation of who he is; faithfully studying it is one of the ways God allows us to know him. The Holy Spirit himself applies this Word to our own lives and situations, giving us wisdom and developing in us unity with Christ and his purposes.

As you've completed this devotional journey together, you have read many Scripture passages with wisdom that can be applied to marriage. Do any of those passages stand out in your memory? (Skim over past weeks if you need to.) How has your relationship changed as you've applied those Scriptures to your life?

—— Day 5 ——

Reflect for a moment on this amazing passage:

> We have not received the spirit of the world but the Spirit who is from God, that we may understand what God has freely given us. This is what we speak, not in words taught us by human wisdom but in words taught by the Spirit, expressing spiritual truths in spiritual words. The man without the Spirit does not accept the things that come from the Spirit of God, for they are foolishness to him, and he cannot understand them, because they are spiritually discerned. The spiritual man makes judgments about all things, but he himself is not subject to any man's judgment: "For who has known the mind of the Lord that he may instruct him?" But we have the mind of Christ. (1 Cor. 2:12–16)

What an astounding truth! We have received the Spirit of God so that we may understand the gift of God—salvation through Christ. We have the Spirit that we may understand the gospel. When we read Scripture, we are not simply reading man's thoughts about God—we are reading "words taught by the Spirit . . . spiritual truths in spiritual words" (v. 13).

If we didn't have the Spirit, we couldn't understand the mind of Christ, because his thoughts are so far beyond our own. But through the Spirit, we have the mind of Christ! And as the Spirit opens our eyes to the truth of God's Word and applies it to our lives, we walk in unity with Christ. Has the Spirit opened your eyes in any way during these past weeks of study? In what ways do you feel that having the "mind of Christ" affects your view of marriage and your spouse?

Christ has called us to have marriages characterized by unity and mutual care. We experience unity as we come to know our spouses more fully. We care for each other as we apply that knowledge to create greater fulfillment in each other. We pray that you will continue to grow in your love for each other, and that as you understand each other, meet each other's basic needs, and encourage one another daily with the hope of the gospel, you will experience romantic love that lasts a lifetime—God's gift to those who follow his plan for their lives.

PRAYER FOR THE WEEK

Lord, thank you for our marriage. We want to walk in unity with each other, and we want to walk in unity with you. We want to know you better and walk with you more faithfully. And please help us to understand each other—our thoughts, ideas, hopes, dreams—so we can walk in deeper unity too. Help us to apply the things we have learned so our marriage will be a reflection of our love for you. Use us to remind each other of your gospel, and of the hope we have in you. Thank you for loving us, saving us, and giving us each other. Amen.

Willard F. Harley, Jr. is a nationally acclaimed clinical psychologist, a marriage counselor, and the bestselling author of numerous books, including *His Needs, Her Needs, Five Steps to Romantic Love, Love Busters,* and *His Needs, Her Needs for Parents*. His popular website www.marriagebuilders.com offers practical solutions to almost any marital problem.

Joyce S. Harley has twenty-five years of radio experience as a talk show host and a producer. She is a recording artist with an active Bible teaching and singing ministry.

Dr. Harley and his wife, Joyce, host a daily radio call-in show, *Marriage Builders*. They live in White Bear Lake, Minnesota.

THE BEST BOOK ON MARRIAGE IS NOW BETTER THAN EVER!

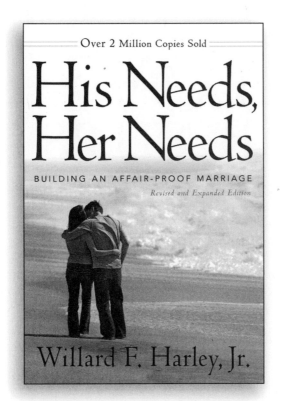

The millions of couples who have read *His Needs, Her Needs* have learned how to keep their romance alive. Join those who have seen spectacular changes in their marriages by following Dr. Harley's tried and proven counsel. You will discover that an outstanding marriage can be more than a dream—it can be your reality.

Are you *losing the love* you once felt for each other?

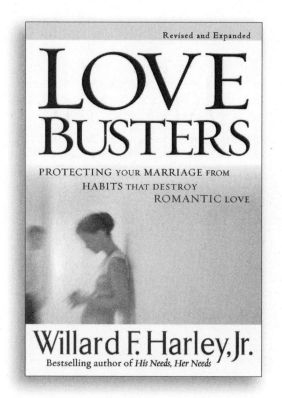

From Dr. Harley, the author of *His Needs, Her Needs*, comes a book that will help you identify the six Love Busters that pull marriages apart, and will show you and your spouse how to avoid them. The strength of your marriage depends on the passion you share for each other. So stop destroying the feeling of love and discover, instead, how to build your love with care and with time.

The best marriage workbook
just got better!

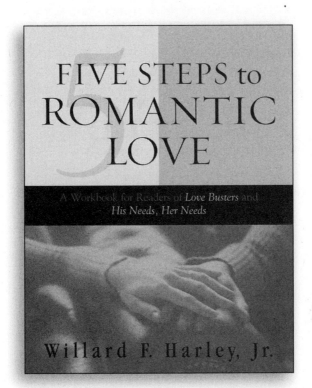

Five Steps to Romantic Love will help you and your spouse to know and meet each other's needs and overcome the habits that destroy your love. This workbook is a supplement to Dr. Harley's *Love Busters* and *His Needs, Her Needs*—books that have helped countless couples fall in love again and enjoy intimate, passionate marriages.

You can have it all—happy children and a thriving marriage.

It isn't easy to keep a marriage passionate. And with children underfoot it can seem downright impossible. Dr. Harley gives you the tools you need to meet two important goals: staying in love and helping your children thrive.

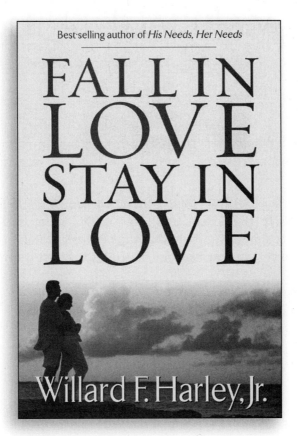

MARRIAGE BUILDERS®

Building Marriages To Last A Lifetime

At MarriageBuliders.com, Dr. Harley introduces you to the best ways to overcome marital conflicts and quickest way to restore love.

Read Dr. Harley's articles, follow the Q&A columns, interact with other couples on the Forum, and listen to Dr. Harley and his wife Joyce answer your questions on Marriage Builders® Radio. Learn to become an expert in making your marriage the best it can be.

Let Marriage Builders® help you build a marriage to last a lifetime!
www.marriagebuilders.com